THE ULTIMATE GUIDE TO NETWORK MARKETING

How to double your income, work part time and become financially independent

Nathan Sloan

NATHAN SLOAN

Copyright © 2020 Nathan Sloan

All rights reserved.

TABLE OF CONTENTS

Introduction 5

PART 1: 7

Why Network Marketing? 7

My Story 7

The 3 Ways To Start a Business 10

What Is Network Marketing? 12

How Does Network Marketing Work? 12

How Network Marketing First Began 16

Why Network Marketing? 18

Living in the New Information Age 18

10 Reasons Why Network Marketing and Why Right Now 19

The 5 Biggest Myths of Multi Level Marketing 24

The 3 Step Plan To Financial Independence 32

What Exactly IS Business? 36

Part 2: 47

How To Build a Successful Business 47

The 3 Pillars 47

The 5 Step System – The Big Picture 52

The 7 Habits of Highly Successful Network Marketers 54

Building Your Franchise 57

- The 3 Stages of a Network Marketing Business.....60
- What You Need To Know About Leadership 63
- What You Need To Know About Marketing.........67
- Who—> What—> How..72
- 5 Ways To Generate More Leads Than You Can Handle 77
- 8 Ways To Get More People Saying, Yes! 82
- What You Need To Know About Sales...................88
- The Inner Game of Sales and Wealth......................91
- The Fortune is in the Follow-Up 104
- How To Handle Objections and FAQ's.................106

Part 3: 110

Turning Pro 110

- The 3 Biggest Mistakes New Network Marketers Make...113
- 5 Steps To Managing Your Time Effectively 114
- The Business Athlete Training System...................120
- Are You An Amateur or Professional? 125
- I wish you happiness & success................................132
- The 5 Best Books for Network Marketers 134

Introduction

I am very excited to be sharing with you business principles that have literally not just changed my life, but have been responsible for making millions of pounds for companies that I have worked for, and for giving me, my financial independence.

What I will be revealing in the following pages, is a combination of over one hundred books, courses and seminars that I have paid thousands of pounds to attend and hundreds of hours to learn.

You have in your hands right now, the finished result. This book is the culmination of all the most valuable tips and secrets all laid out ready for you to discover and capitalise on.

You will notice that this book is quite short, and I have done so for a specific reason.

I did not want to create hundreds of pages of fluff that you get in many other books.

I have been ruthless with the content, deleting large chunks from the original version, and I have only kept in the "essential information" that has been designed to move you from where you are right now, to where you want to be.

Throughout history, there are brief moments in time where several things all come together at once, and a doorway opens up to reveal incredible opportunity.

You may not realise this yet, however, right now, is such a moment.

This is a very exciting time to be alive, and there has never been a better time in history to be building a network marketing business. You are in an incredibly fortunate place to be reading this book right now.

I have been very fortunate to have had 1-1 business coaching from some of the world's most successful business owners, combine this with the recent rise of the Internet, making it easier than ever before to connect with hundreds of people, and it all means you are absolutely in the right place at the absolute right time.

In fifty years from now, you will either look back and thank your lucky stars you came to realise this and be living the life that you have always known was possible for yourself, or you will be kicking yourself that you did not take action on what I am about to share with you.

The choice is yours.

I look forward to hearing your success story one day.

You are about to embark on an amazing journey.

PART 1:

Why Network Marketing?

My Story

I wasn't fortunate enough to come from a privileged background. I was brought up in a place where if you were making more than £30,000 a year, you were classed as doing very well.

I really didn't do too well in school either. I was never good at "following the rules" or working hard because all I wanted to do was to go outside and play games with friends.

The big turning point in my life came when I was working as a professional singer. I was 28 years old and making 'OK money,' but I knew I could be doing better. And so, I began reading for the first time in my life.

Up until that point, I had not read a single book. It was at this time that I began learning about money.

It was a very exciting time as I began uncovering all kinds of "secrets" from successful business owners and millionaires all about money and investing, and what I was learning really shocked me.

I remember thinking, why did I not get taught this at school?

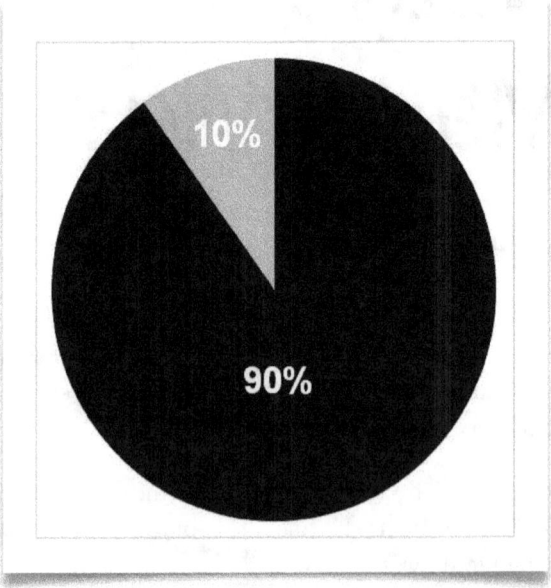

Figure 1: 90% Vs 10%

Here is one of the principles which I found fascinating:

> **I learned that 90% of the population are employees and the self-employed, who are "selling their time for money."**
>
> **They work in the system which means, when they work, they get paid, but, when they don't go to work, <u>they don't get paid</u>.**

Now, this is OK in the short term, but it is terrible in the medium and long term.

Why is this?

This is because you can <u>never stop working</u>. As an employee, or self-employed person, you are tied to your income. It is like a one-legged chair. If you take that leg away, your entire life comes tumbling down.

The other point that I found out about this way of making money is that it is really hard to become wealthy. This is because there are only 24 hours in a day and as long as you "sell time for money" you are, therefore, giving your income a limit.

Now, on the flip side, 10% of the population play by a different set of rules. They are business owners. They own "a system" that people are working for.

They do not work for a paycheck, they work for profit.

I discovered a fact that 93% of millionaires own a business.

Now, I could not believe what I was learning. Why was I not told this?

I continued on. The big benefit to owning your own business is that you can create an income that doesn't require you to be there.

This was amazing news!

The problem was, I didn't know anything about business.

I did know that business was obviously the smart way to earn a living and what I should be doing, but where did I even begin?

The 3 Ways To Start a Business

I found out that there were only "three ways" in which you can start and own your own business.

The first option was by building a "Traditional Business."

This is where you start from scratch. You have to create a brand, logo, design, product or service, do the sales, marketing, advertising, distribution, customer service, accounts just to name a few parts of what makes up a successful business.

As I didn't have any experience at this time, it did seem quite a risky way to get started as there was so much that could go wrong (and way too much work than I could handle).

The second way to start a business was to "Buy a Franchise."

You see franchises every day on the high street like Starbucks, McDonalds and Specsavers. This is a fantastic option because 90% of the work has already been done.

Someone else has already gone through the hard part of spending years of time and tens of thousands of pounds doing all the hard work, all you have to do is to plug in and go. Excellent.

The problem, which I later discovered, is that it requires a large upfront investment to buy a licence, and the monthly costs of running a business are thousands of pounds for shop rent, staff and stock, etc.

Many of the top franchises required £100,000+ just to get started.

Now, I didn't have that kind of money, and the thought of getting a bank loan again just seemed too risky.

What if it didn't work out? I would really be in trouble.

This is when I first saw the words, network marketing.

I didn't even know what it was. I have never heard of it

before. So I began my due diligence and here is what I discovered.

What Is Network Marketing?

Network marketing is a way for anyone, regardless of age, gender, experience or background, to start a business and become financially independent.

The business is very similar to a franchise, where 90% of the work has already been done; however, unlike a franchise, it doesn't require a large upfront investment.

This was it. Once I learned this, I knew that this was how I was going to become a business owner and become financially free.

How Does Network Marketing Work?

There are basically two main ways of getting products to customers. There is "Traditional Retail," where the products get made by the manufacturer, they are then bought at 'wholesale' and sold at 'retail' normally through a shop.

Traditional business

The other way of getting products to customers is through network marketing. This is where the products are made by the manufacturer (which is normally the actual network marketing company) and then shipped directly to the customer, cutting out the retail stores.

Network marketing

The difference with this way of doing business is that the end customer can also become what is known as an "Independent Consultant."

What is an independent consultant?

This is someone who can build a business by recommending the companies products and taking a percentage of the sales they make.

One of the benefits with the network marketing distribution model, is that it cuts out the middleman, which means that the companies have more money which they then invest in making better quality products.

Network marketing products, in general, are higher quality than you will find on the high street.

What most of the population doesn't realise is that the prime focus of a traditional business is to make a profit, so what happens is that more money is spent on marketing and advertising the products than is actually spent on the products themselves.

You may not know this yet, but many of the products on

the high street and supermarkets are being mixed with cheap "bulking agents" and "chemicals" which give the products a longer shelf life. This means they can be sold to the mass market, meaning you and me.

So the problem is that many of these products being bought and sold are actually not very good for you.

"If this is such a good way of doing business, why has network marketing got a bit of a bad reputation?"

Unfortunately, as anyone can start a business without any experience, this does cause a problem.

It means there are thousands of new "Business Owners" who haven't had any business or sales experience. This leads to people trying to "Sell" to every person they meet with a pulse.

Over the decades, this has caused a lot of people to have a bad experience with network marketing and has given the industry a tainted name.

However, the good news is that you do not need to run your business like this, I will show you how to avoid this scenario later.

"I have heard that 90% of businesses fail, So why would I even bother trying?"

It is true that most people who start a business are not successful, but we must also understand that this is *everywhere* in life, not just in business.

Let me explain.

How many people join a gym at the start of the year, with the intention of getting into the best shape of their life? And how many, end up quitting within 6 months? It's also about 90% right?

Here is another example.

How many people will start a martial arts class to become a black belt, and how many do you think will quit before becoming a master?

It's about 90% right?

Now, does this mean that you should not try to get a good body, or start in martial arts or any other sport or skill?

Of course not. Anyone can do it, but you just need to start in the right way and get access to the right mentors and training from the beginning.

I personally find it funny that people are happy to spent money on the national lottery, where the odds are around 14,000,000:1 yet, they do not even try to start a business, where the odds are 10:1.

These are actually great odds. Just go in to the city centre on a weekend and count the 1:10s. There will be a hundred in the shopping centre alone, and this too can be you.

> **The lesson:** Do not listen to people who say it can't be done. 1:10 is great odds.

How Network Marketing First Began

Network marketing (also known as multi level marketing or MLM) is a massive industry which generates over £150 billion every year.

There are over 90 million people all around the world involved, and tens of thousands more getting involved each year.

It all began back in the 1930s with a man named Carl Rehnborg. Whilst working in China, between 1917 and 1927, Mr Rehnborg was first introduced to the benefits of using supplements in his diet, and the additional health benefits that it gave people.

When Carl got back to America, he set up his own company called "The California Vitamin Company." In 1939, he re-branded the company as "Nutrilite."

It wasn't until 6 years later that Carl invented the multi level marketing strategy to help boost the sales of his company.

It was around this time that two new consultants, Jay Van Andel and Rich DeVos became distributors of the Nutrilite products, and they quickly noticed the real power of this business model as sales were growing at an exponential rate.

They set up a competing company called Amway and bought a controlling interest in Nutrilite in 1972. In 1994, Amway then took over full ownership and is now one of the largest network marketing companies.

It is amazing to think that the multi-level marketing business model is not even one hundred years old yet. It is only just now starting to get going.

Why Network Marketing?

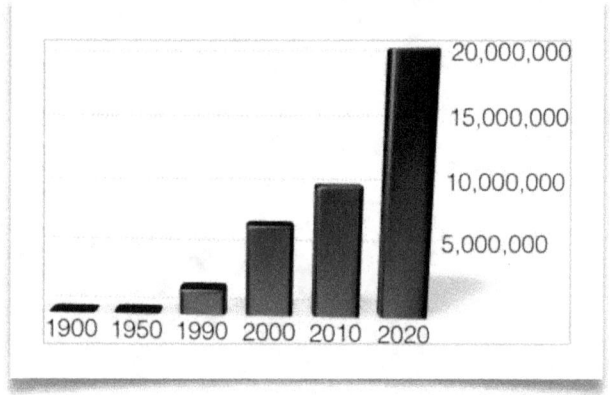

Figure 2: Millionaires Worldwide - source: Merrill Lynch

I strongly believe that building a network marketing business is one of the smartest things you can do with your time and money in today's economy.

To be successful in network marketing, it is important to understand why you should even bother, as the truth is that it does take time and serious effort to build a business and will likely be one of the most challenging things you have done with your life so far.

Most people are quite comfortable with where they are, so why bother?

Living in the New Information Age

For the last 2000 years of human history we lived in what was called the "Agrarian Age". This was when business and wealth was all about farming. Whoever owned the farms and the land controlled the wealth.

In the 20th Century, we moved in to a new age called the "Industrial Age." The big corporate giants like Andrew Carnegie and Henry Ford, with their steel and car companies dominated the business world. In the Industrial Age, it was whoever owned the factories that controlled the wealth.

From the year 2000 onwards, however, with the rise of the Internet, we are now living in a new age. "The Information Age." Today, companies like Twitter and Facebook are changing the world.

Today it is all about building and owning "Networks" that is what creates wealth.

The Internet has levelled the playing field. Today, it has never been easier or a better time in all of history to build and own a business.

See figure 2. There are more people becoming millionaires right now than in any other time in history. Are you going to take advantage and be one of them?

10 Reasons Why Network Marketing and Why Right Now

1. Financial Freedom

The ultimate reason to have your own business is so that you can own your own life. It means having an income that does not require you to be there, so you can do all the things that you want to do with your life.

It means not being trapped in the 9-5 Rat Race, only to retire in 30 years from now on the equivalent of minimum wage.

2. Build Your Fortune, Not Someone Else's

When you go to work each day and put in your eight hours, who is earning a paycheck and who is building a fortune?

The smart people are now waking up and spending their time building their <u>own</u> fortune, not someone else's. It is said that the people without goals are destined to work for those who do.

3. Great Incentives

Does the company that you currently work for really look after their best people? Do they buy them luxury cars if they do well? Do they pay for them to go on 5* luxury holidays?

Do they regularly buy them luxury gifts to say thank you for all their hard work? Because the top network marketing companies do.

4. Utilise Tax Incentives Used by the Rich

As soon as you start your own business, even if it just part time, you get to utilise the same tax breaks that rich people use.

Did you know, the average person pays 30-50% in income tax alone. A business owner can easily pay up to 40% less in tax. You can get tax deductions on many items including your office, equipment, rent, travel, just to name a few.

With a business, it is a double benefit. You can earn more money and pay less in tax, leaving more money in your bank account.

5. Benefit by Using Premium Products

By using your new company's products, you also get the additional benefit of using really high quality products.

If you are with a health and wellness company for example, you would enjoy great looking skin, higher energy throughout the day, improved nutrition, living a longer life, which also improves confidence and self esteem.

6. Utilise This Time in History or Kick Yourself

As you have seen, there has never been a better time in history to build a fortune with a business.

The introduction of the Internet will only happen once. You now have access to the best tools, companies, people, resources and everything else that you will ever need. All you have to do is to realise this and go out and take action.

7. A £10,000 Personal Development Program

Another reason this business model is becoming so popular is because it is in everyone's best interest to help you become as successful as you can be.

It is a win/win/win. The more money you make, the more your sponsor makes which in turn, the more money the company makes.

This is why you are given the very best training in business, sales, marketing and leadership. You are in a 'no lose' situation, whether you become success in this business or not. You can only gain.

8. *Retire in 3-5 Years (not 50)*

Our current system is set up so that we graduate from university now with between £30K-£50K of debt, we work for fifty years, only to retire on the equivalent of minimum wage.

With a network marketing business, you get the opportunity to work and retire, on more money, and after only 3-5 years of hard work, and people are starting to realise this.

9. *Make a Real Difference To People's Lives*

One of the biggest hidden gems of this business that most people are not even aware of is that you are developing and helping other people become the best they can be.

It is incredibly rewarding to know that your work is making a real difference in people's lives and you are being recognised for all the work you do. You are literally changing people's lives for the better, building them up and sharing their successes and making the world a better place.

10. Utilise The Population Boom

It is not just millionaires that are growing at an exponential rate, world population is also going off the charts. (see Figure 1-3)

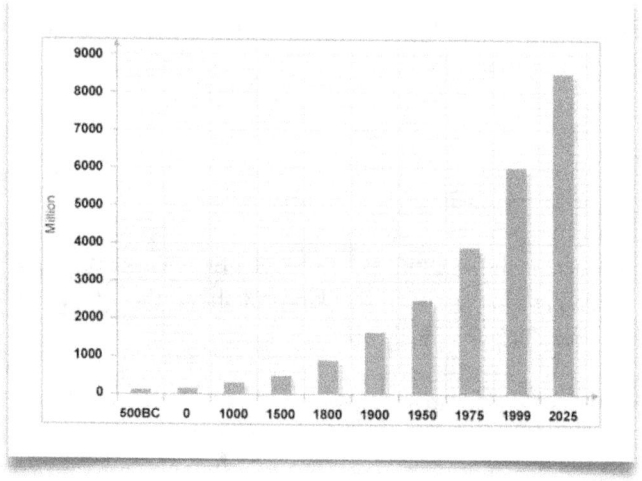

Figure 3: The Current Population Boom

Why is this important?

Well, some companies like car companies for example, were not built to thrive in this new economy.

What will happen is that our roads will begin to get gridlocked and full of pollution, whereas, a network marketing business is set to do <u>better</u> with more people as it is a people based business.

In the years and decades to come, which business would you like to own?

The 5 Biggest Myths of Multi Level Marketing

I am now going to go head on with the most common myths regarding network marketing.

Let me start with what I think is the biggest problem with this profession and why 95% of these misunderstandings exist.

It is because most people who start in MLM have <u>never had any previous business experience</u>.

This means that the industry is full of untrained sales people, running around and saying all kinds of things they shouldn't be saying. This is actually causing a lot of problems.

Why does this happen?

It is because it is very common when first starting out in business to only think about making money and to only think about your own needs, problems and wants, and not to consider other people so much.

The vast majority of people are just trying to make sales in any way they know how.

But this is not how good business works, and this is why we now have some misunderstandings.

Myth 1. Pyramid Structures Are A Bad Thing

The first biggest misunderstanding people have with this type of business, is that just because it has a pyramid structure, it must be bad.

Some brand new, inexperienced consultants do not know how to respond to this comment and may try to deny it or cover it up, but here is the correct response.

So what if it does?

The important point to note is that so does traditional business, and government, and religion and nearly every big organisation that contains lots of people.

All big organisations have a pyramid structure.

In traditional business, you have the CEO at the top, followed by heads of department, followed by upper management, followed by middle management, followed by lower management, followed by supervisors, followed by staff members and finally all the customers.

Let's take religion. In Christianity, for example, you have the Pope at the top, followed by cardinals, followed by priests, followed by church leaders, followed by helpers and so on.

In government, you have the President or Prime Minister that sits at the top, followed by their closest advisors, followed by heads of department, followed by chief MPs, followed by MPs and so on.

As you can see, this is everywhere.

Remember This: Pyramid structures are a strong structure that is proven to build any type of organisation.

Myth 2. Isn't MLM A Scam?

Another concern people have about starting a network marketing business is that they have heard that it might be a scam or a pyramid scheme.

If this was you, then do not worry. Firstly, MLM is not a scam or pyramid scheme.

Why? Simply because pyramid schemes are illegal.

What Is A Pyramid Scheme?

A pyramid scheme is where the owner of the scheme gets people to invest their money, with the hope of getting a return on their investment.

Now, the owner keeps recruiting new people, and then begins to pay off the initial people with the new investors' money.

The main difference is that there is <u>no product involved</u>. The product is essentially just <u>money</u>.

Pyramid schemes are illegal. The big difference is that MLM distributes actual products and are not illegal.

The industry is regulated by a strict government body that has been around for decades, and network marketing is one of the fastest growing industries of today.

The reason you may have heard it being a scam is because someone will have joined a company, realised that there was actual work involved and then probably quit.

To save face, they then tell their friends and family that it was just a scam and they get to save on any embarrassment of not looking like a failure.

It is now used as an excuse more than anything else.

Myth 3. The Numbers Don't Add Up

The next concern is that the numbers in network marketing don't add up.

If this was true, then why is the industry doing better now than ever before?

The main argument comes from companies teaching the system of finding 4 people who find 4 people and so on. This is the compounding growth model. It works like this.

4

16

64

256

1024

4096

16,384

65,536

262,144

1,048,576

And so on. The problem people have with this is that it is

not mathematically possible for this to continue, as you would run out of people in the world. (The critics love mentioning this.)

Here is the important point. This is not how network marketing must be done.

This is <u>just an example</u> of how you can grow a business using only referrals.

This is the same example you could give <u>any</u> business, not just this one.

You can build a very successful network marketing business without <u>ever recruiting anyone</u>.

If you want, you can just get customers, like any other business.

We just teach the build 4 find 4 strategy because it is a really easy concept for a brand new person to understand and get started with.

Which leads me nicely to my next point.

It's Easy To Be A Critic

It's so easy to be a critic. Anyone can be a critic. Anyone can sit there and pick faults in people and businesses and tell you all the reasons why it won't work.

What is more difficult (and admirable) is not to just 'follow the crowd' and actually stand up for something you believe in.

Going for your dreams and putting yourself out there in front of this type of criticism is commendable.

There are two kinds of people in this world. Ones that go out and push to build a better life for themselves and their families, and the people who just sit there, poke faults and tell you all the reasons why it can't be done.

Myth 4. What About The Ethics and Relationship Costs?

Now we come to the point of whether this business has ethical or relationship costs when talking with family and friends.

The problem <u>isn't the business,</u> the problem is HOW you build your business.

If you had a way of genuinely improving the lives of the closest loved ones around you, then you would be doing them a disservice by not letting them know about it.

If that person wasn't interested, then fine.

There are millions of people becoming financially independent all around the world with network marketing.

The industry is one of the fastest growing there is right now that has created more millionaires than any other industry, fact.

You would actually be annoyed with your friend if you became a big success and you hadn't told them about it and given them the freedom of choice to decide whether it was right for them or not.

So the actual problem is not the business. The problem is HOW people get told.

The problem is when people do things like 'trick' their friends into hearing about it. They might ask them to meet up for a catch up and then suddenly launch into their glorious business opportunity.

DO NOT DO THIS.

This is why people think there might be relationship costs. It is not good for anyone, and this is what is giving the industry a bad name. If this is you then, don't do it.

> **Bottom Line:** Just be open and honest, and let people decide for themselves if this is right for them or not, and there will be no relationship costs.

Myth 5. Only The People At The Top Ever Make Any Money

The next concern people have, is that it is only the people at the top that make any money.

They will tell you that 90% of people who join don't make any money, so what's the point?

Guess what? This is true. They are right. However, as we saw in an earlier chapter, this is also true for many other things.

You can become a black belt in the martial arts, and you can go to the gym and get in the best shape of your life.

It is just not going to be given to you on a plate. You are going to have to work for it, likely over a number of years.

> **Here is the Good News**
>
> If you do take it seriously, if you do set clear goals, if you do turn up to training every time, if you do get better every day, if you do have strong reasons why you are doing this, then you too can and will be in the top 10% of people.
>
> That's all they did.

The 3 Step Plan To Financial Independence

I am going to share with you a very simple, but very powerful life coaching exercise for designing the life you want to be living.

The time you spend on this short exercise will save you decades of time later on.

I learned this from a very successful multi-millionaire, and I am now passing this on to you.

The truth is that the reason people do not get what they want is because they have not taken the time to find what it is they actually want.

Most people go through life following what everyone else is doing and getting caught up in the tide.

They do not just, STOP, sit down and plan what they actually want their life to be like.

We, as humans, are the only species which doesn't just have to live in stimulus and response. We have the freedom of choice.

This is about getting really clear on where your life is right now (situation), which is different for every one of us, what you would actually life your life to be like (the destination) and then exactly how you are going to get there (the vehicle).

A wise man once said to me that you must start with the

life you want to create, and then, build a business to support that life.

Most people make the mistake of starting a business which then consumes them and becomes their life. This not why we want a business.

Step 1: The Situation
Where are you right now?

This is the starting point. It all starts with your current situation, which is where you are right now.

Now, this is the part that is unique to everyone. Everyone starts from a different place. We all have different backgrounds, different upbringings, different experiences to draw upon.

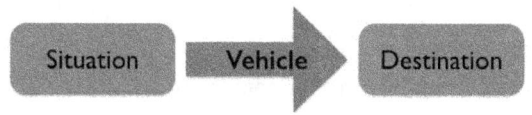

The important point is that it doesn't matter where you are at right now. There have been other people in the world who have had less than you have right now, who have become successful.

There have been people who have had less money, more children, worked more hours, even have fewer limbs on their body. Everyone's journey is unique.

Here are the 3 questions you need to answer to design the life you want.

How can you create at least 10-20 hours per week to build your business?

How can you do 30-60 minutes of exercise each day?

How can you create a supportive environment while you build your business?

Once you have established where you are in life right now, it is time to get clear on where it is you would like to be. This is your destination.

Step 2: The Destination
What does the end result look like?

You would never get in a car or go to the airport without first knowing your destination, right? Yet this is how most people are living their lives.

They are just drifting in day-to-day issues and then wonder why they do not have all the things they want. It's nothing short of crazy.

You now need a <u>clear picture</u> of what you would like your life to be like. Once we have this critical information, we can then build a plan of how to make it a reality. It really is that simple.

Write answers to the following questions.

How much money would you like to be making each month?

How many hours a day would you like to work?

What would you do with your free time?

Where would you like to live, and what car would you drive?

How many holidays would you go on each year and where to?

Knowing this, I want you to ask yourself, if you kept on doing what you are doing right now and you didn't change anything in your life, is this where you are going?

For most people, it is not.

This is the reason why we can build a business. It is one of the best vehicles to use to create the life you want. Thousands of people from all walks of life are doing this, and so can you.

You probably just have not had access to this type of training before. Well, now you do. It's your turn.

Step 3: The Vehicle
How are you going to get there?

The final step is the vehicle, which is about <u>how</u> you are going to get from A to B.

Most people are using a job as their vehicle, but if your job isn't going to get you where you actually want to go, it is time to use a better vehicle.

This is your business.

Network marketing is just a better vehicle for getting you from A to B. That's it. Now, it is not perfect, but it is better.

What Exactly IS Business?

Before you can get started building a business, you need to fully understand what exactly business is.

Businesses are everywhere. They are on nearly every street. They create all the jobs. They create a large portion of the taxes.

There are big ones, small ones, people want to be "in business" and you will probably have heard many stories about business and business people.

But what exactly IS business and why do we have them?

Think about this for a second because I am about to change how you think about business from now on.

Now, when I ask people this question, I normally get answers like, it is about selling products and services, or it is about finding and keeping customers, or it is about making money, right?

Now all of these answers are a 'part' of business, but they are not what a business is.

We must understand exactly what business is and why we have them, as this will then give you the best chance of creating a successful one.

Makes sense?

Side Point: I want to state that you should not be scared or intimidated about business. Business is a <u>learnable skill,</u> and everyone starts from the same place, knowing nothing and having nothing.

All you need is the <u>desire to learn</u>.

Key Concept 1: Businesses solve problems and make your life better in some way.

You need to start thinking about business and products in terms of "problems" and "solutions." Businesses solve problems and thereby, make your life better.

Look around the room right now and notice all the products around you.

Let's take, a table for example.

So what is the problem that this product solves?

Well, if tables didn't exist, then you would have to eat and work on the floor right? This would be really uncomfortable.

By inventing the table, you can now eat and work in more comfort and increase your productivity. Problem solved and your life is now better.

What you don't see is that there is a "business" behind every table that creates and distributes them.

Let's do another example so that this really sinks in as it is important.

Let's take a car for example.

What problem does this product solve?

Well, before cars it would take you weeks to travel across the country on horseback. This was not only time consuming but very uncomfortable.

With the invention of the car, you can now double, triple or quadruple your speed and travel in more comfort too. It's a great business that solves an important problem and thereby makes your life better.

Understand?

Last example.

A network marketing business.

What problem does owning a network marketing business solve?

Well, our current working system involves graduating university, now with £30K-£50K of debt, working for fifty years until 67, only to retire on the equivalent of minimum wage.

If you have never really stopped and thought about this, it's not a great way to live.

This is a really serious problem many people have, wouldn't you agree?

Now, a network marketing business gives you the opportunity to retire, debt free, in 3-5 years, and, retire on <u>more</u> money than you were previously making.

This solves that problem, and your life is now better off for it.

> **Bottom Line:** All businesses solve problems. As a business owner, you are a "problem solver." This is a very important point.

Why am I telling you this?

Because, when it comes to speaking with people, there is a massive difference between solving that person's problems and you just trying to make money from them. More on this later.

Key Concept 2: The more people a business helps or serves, then the more money the business makes.

The next concept to understand is what determines how much money a business makes.

The rule of thumb is that the more people the business helps, the more money the business will make.

Let's take a quick look at a couple of businesses to help this concept sink in.

The Children's Lemonade Stand

Picture This: It's a hot day. You have been walking for a few hours, and you are dehydrated.

You then spot a lemonade stand in your street, being run by your next door neighbour's children.

They offer you a delicious beverage and at a great price. You drink your lemonade that was served to you with a warm smile, and you now feel better.

Remember concept one? Your life has been improved at a good price. Everybody is happy.

Even though this is a very small micro-business, just note that this business still has income, expenses, products, suppliers, customer service and is a business (and a great way to learn solid business principles).

However, as this business only serves a handful of people in the street, it only has a small market to serve and so will only make a small amount of money.

The Virgin Group

Virgin, created by Richard Branson, is an example of a big business. This business in contrast, helps millions of people travel across the world faster and in comfort.

It also helps thousands of people travel across the country and have access to super fast Internet, which as you will agree, solves a really important problem.

This is why this business makes millions of pounds each year. It's a massive market helping lots of people.

Make sense?

What Business Is NOT

I think it is also important to cover what business is not.

Real business is not about ripping people off. Business is not about "getting one over" on someone. Business is not about tricking someone into buying something that they don't want or need.

Although there are businesses out there that do that, this is not what real business is about.

So, you now know exactly what business is, we can move on to getting started with your own business. Let's continue.

Key Concept 3: The best businesses are built on a strong mission

You will notice that the best businesses in the world have been built on a strong mission that goes beyond just making money.

Rich Dad Mission

To elevate the financial wellbeing of humanity.

Apple Inc Mission

Apple is committed to bringing the best personal computing experience to students, educators, creative professionals and consumers around the world through its innovative hardware, software and Internet offerings.

Amazon Mission

Our vision is to be earth's most customer centric company; to build a place where people can come to find and discover anything they might want to buy online.

In network marketing, you are helping people transition from "selling time for money" as employees, to becoming financially independent as successful business owners.

Managing Expectations

We all want to get rich quickly. I know I did. I get it.

The truth is though (which most of the "gurus" out there are too scared to tell you) that business is like any other profession.

It takes time. It takes time to learn and develop the skills that you need to make your business a success.

What I find interesting is that if you wanted to become an accountant, or builder or a professional golfer or anything else, you naturally except that the initial training could take anywhere from 1-4 years, and there would be costs involved.

Yet for some reason, people expect to be making a lot of money in business within their first six months, even though they have no experience and have not done any training courses.

So why do we do this?

There is a couple of reasons. The first is that many network marketers are too scared to tell you that you

might not make a lot of money right away because then, you might not join their team, so people "bend the truth."

The second reason is that we always hear stories about people who did make lots of money in their first year. So surely you should too, right?

> **Remember this:** 5% of people, which is about 1 in 20 of us, do make money quickly.

There are several reasons for this. They may have an excellent network, they may have had previous business experience, or they just work like an absolute dog.

However, the worst thing you can do is compare yourself with the 5% because, for most people, 19 out of 20 in fact, this isn't their reality.

This is one of the main reasons why people quit in their

first year, they get disheartened by comparing themselves with these people, when in fact, even if you do not make a penny in your first year, you are absolutely on track to becoming widely successful.

Training For Your Black Belt

The best comparison I can give you to help you understand what it takes to become successful in business is like training to become a black belt in the martial arts.

It requires you to start with the right expectations, turn up for training, day in day out and consistently keep pushing yourself to the next level.

Again, 1 in 20 people will do it faster because they may have had experience in other martial arts already or have a physical advantage, but, anyone can do it with consistent work. We all start from different places.

You have to <u>learn the skills</u> and then drill them over and over and over until they become a habit.

"Business is not something you just 'try' for a few months, business is a <u>life choice</u>."

Business is not just something you try out for six month and see if it works for you. This is why most people fail.

The truth is that business is a medium to long term plan.

Let's get some perspective.

A job is actually great in the short term. You do a little bit of work for a month, and then you get paid. Excellent.

But, in the medium to long term, it is awful. This is

because you can never stop working without your income suddenly stopping. You are destined to work for the rest of your life.

A business is the opposite. In the short term, for most people it is not great. It requires a lot of work, without much money, which is why most people quit.

But, in the medium to long term, it is excellent. It creates massive wealth and abundance, and you can build an income that does not require you to be there.

The Exponential Power Curve

One of the most valuable principles that you learn and understand is the principle of "Exponential Growth." Otherwise known as "Compounding." It looks like this.

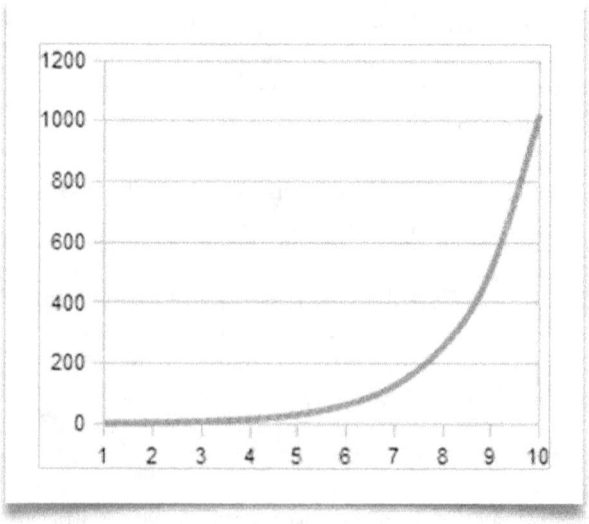

Figure 4 - Business income for a beginner

Figure 4 shows what the typical business income will look like when you first start out in business. This gives you a visual of why 90% of people quit.

They quit before they reach point 5 on the chart where all their hard work and training begins to pay off and compound.

The reason most people quit is because we have been trained for decades to be "employees," so when all of a sudden we are not getting paid for our work, it becomes too painful and we quit.

How fast you travel up this curve depends on you. It depends on how many hours you put in and how hard you work. It is said to take 10,000 hours to master any skill. If you want 10x the income as the average person, you are simply going to have to pay your dues. All champions are made in training.

Not many people realise that most of the top business experts in the world failed miserably for a couple of years before they got good This includes people like Sir Richard Branson, the best there is.

This is why it is <u>so important</u> to have the attitude of, I will do this "until it works" not, I will give it a try "to see" if it works.

PART 2:

How To Build a Successful Business

The 3 Pillars

This is the starting point for your business. We are going to be looking at the three pillars.

Each of these pillars is a crucial element which will help you clarify your destination and answer the most important question.

Why are you doing this?

The third pillar is how to reprogram your brain for success.

Pillar I – Your Vision

The first pillar is your <u>vision</u>.

What is your vision?

Your vision is having a clear picture in your mind of what the end result is.

You write out your destination in the previous chapter, now is the time to take this and visualise what your life is going to be like when you have achieved it.

There is a very good reason why top athletes, in all disciplines, visualise their performance before they do it.

There is a reason why top salespeople visualise their presentations going excellently before they actually do it.

It is because visualisation <u>works</u>.

You are literally programming your brain with what you want to happen.

It utilises the "Law of Attraction," which states that whatever you think about, you are expanding and are actually bringing into your life.

The most successful people in the world are "Visionaries." They clearly saw what they wanted in their minds, long before they achieved it, whether they did this purposely or not.

Your vision needs to be so crystal clear that you can see it, feel it and hear it.

This is the end result. This is what you are building a business for. This is the lifestyle you are going to create. As you can see, this is so important.

Write out your vision statement. Which is when you have achieved your vision, what will your life be like? How will your day be? How big is your team? How have you changed? What will you now be able to do?

Write this out and then print this out and put it where you can see it every day.

Like everything else, this is just a skill which you can and need to develop.

 Pillar II – Your WHY

The most important question you need answering is:

Why are you building this business?

This is the fundamental key to your motivation. It is what is going to get you through the good days and the bad days when you feel like quitting.

If you have a strong enough why, then you can overcome ANY how.

It's a fact that the people who have the biggest reason why, are the ones that ultimately succeed and the ones who don't, do not.

List the top 10 reasons why you are doing this business. Then, looking at your responses, ask yourself why these are important to you and write those down.

Write all this into a small statement, print it out and also keep it where you can see it <u>every day</u>. Do not skip these steps. They are in here for a very important reason.

Pillar III – Affirmations

Affirmations are going to be your secret weapon that will serve you well, especially in times of need.

What are affirmations?

They are basically a set of words that you say to yourself.

For example, "I can do this."

or

"There is no problem I cannot overcome."

In hypnotherapy, they are known as "Embedded Commands" and have been proven to work.

Now, before you begin thinking this is the fluffy stuff you can skip, the fact is that <u>you already use affirmations</u>. You probably just are not aware that you do.

Let me explain.

If you have ever looked in the mirror and just thought to yourself, "I look tired," this is an affirmation.

If you have ever compared yourself to someone and then said, "Yer, but I am not like that". That is an affirmation.

When you say these things to yourself, you are literally programming your brain to give you more of this result, and then this becomes your reality.

Your affirmations are either helping you or they are

keeping you stuck in life.

The key is to take control of your conditioning and <u>be in control</u> of what you are saying to yourself.

This is a really serious matter. Your success depends on this.

Here is how to take control back.

You create five affirmations to give yourself, that are the opposite of your biggest limiting beliefs.

Here are a list, to give you some examples.

> ***I am full of energy and enthusiasm***
> ***There is no problem I cannot handle***
> ***I am loving life and the challenge it offers***
> ***I am great with all kinds of people***
> ***I can do this. I can and I will***
> ***I am great at public speaking***
> ***I am getting better and better everyday***

The difference between the masses and successful people, is that successful people are using positive affirmations many times, probably without even knowing about it.

They may look in the mirror and say to themselves, "I look really good today".

The 5 Step System – The Big Picture

When it comes down to it, everything you will be doing will fit into one of the following areas:

1. Prospecting
2. Presenting
3. Following Up
4. Sponsoring
5. Repeat and Duplicate

The full process involves prospecting potential partners, presenting the information you have, taking people through a follow up system until they are ready to begin, and then repeating the process and teaching others how to do the same.

This is the big picture. Breaking these down, we see that there are 6 key skills we need to practice and master.

The 6 Key Skills To Master

1. Lead Generation
2. Booking Meetings
3. Presenting The Opportunity
4. Following Up
5. Sponsoring and Launching A New Consultant
6. Teaching and Training

How do we get really good?

To get really good we just need to use the "100 Rule." This states that the first time we do anything we are probably not going to be very good at it.

After 10 attempts, we begin to get OK, and after 100 times, we begin to get really good. So the only way to get really good is by doing each skill 100x and accepting that the first ones are not going to be great.

The Importance of Habits

Now, at this point, you might be asking, OK, I have my plan, I will now be starting with the correct expectations, so tell me, what do I need to do?

The first thing to understand is that everything you have in your life, your current income, your current health and body, your relationships etc., are a result of your current habits.

If you want to have different things or different results in your life, then you are going to need to replace some of them and improve some existing ones.

<u>You</u> must be in control of your habits, and not let your habits control you.

I am now going to show you what 95% of the top earners do each day, week and month. If you build these habits into your life, then you too will get the same results.

The 7 Habits of Highly Successful Network Marketers

Habit 1. The Monthly Requirement

The only fixed monthly expense (overhead) in your business is the monthly requirement which varies slightly from company to company.

This is mandatory and is how network marketing works. If you do not do your monthly requirement, then you are setting your whole organisation up for failure and problems.

It also sends a very strong message to your sponsor that you are not serious about your business and becoming financial independent. This is the starting point.

Habit 2. Present To 3-5 People Each Week

From the words of one of the most successful network marketers in the world, "The person who presents to the most people wins."

If you only did one thing each month, this would be it and is also the one thing you cannot miss.

Our only job is to show people that there is a better way to make a living. A way of working smarter, not harder. Show them it exists, and let them decide for themselves.

Habit 3. Follow Up and Sponsor – 7-10 Exposures

Most people do not join on the first exposure to the presentation. In all businesses, it takes on average, 7-10 exposures or touch points for people to understand what this business actually is. Most of the top earners said 'no' on the first presentation.

It has taken people 20 years to learn a certain way to live life, this isn't going to change in an instant. The fortune and success is in the follow up. A process of adding value, educating, developing and helping people improve their lives.

Habit 4. Daily Personal Development–1-2 Hours

Network marketing isn't hard and it isn't easy, it is what it is. We are the variable. The better we get, the easier it becomes. 1-2 hours of either reading and/or listening to audios keeps you plugged in and you are doing a mental workout for your brain.

Over the weeks and months you will notice incredible benefits that affect every part of your life and the life of your team. Fill that dead commuting time by learning from experts.

This is exactly the same as doing a physical workout in the gym. After the gym, you feel pumped up, and if you do it consistently for long enough, you will look great.

The same is true for your brain. When you listen to audio, it makes you feel great and inspired, and if you keep it up for long enough, your life will begin to change around you.

However, if you stop doing either then your mind gets out of shape, you begin to get fat, negative thoughts take hold and mental weeds begin to grow.

Sharpening The Saw

Prospecting is like chopping down a tree. When first starting out, it is like using a hammer. Hard work, where you feel you are getting nowhere. As you get better, it is like using a saw. It gets easier and easier, the better you get.

Habit 5. Attend All Trainings

Attending all the trainings is a <u>must</u>. It not only makes you into a better consultant, it also helps build and strengthen your team. Enjoy the culture, meet your team and learn from the best.

This business gives you a paid social life. The trainings give your business several benefits that duplicate all the way down your business. This includes phone calls, monthly meetings and big events. All are critical to learn from and duplicate.

Habit 6. Daily Exercise 30-60 Minutes

You may wonder why I have included exercise and diet in the daily activities. Surly this is optional, right? Unfortunately not. You will notice that all the top earners exercise.

The simple fact of the matter is that if you look and feel great, then you will be 100x more effective at everything, including stress management. People will be looking at you and judging whether they want what you have.

Habit 7. Take Your Business Seriously

Your business can give you £100,000 income, working a 4 hour workday and give you financial independence for you and your family for the rest of your life, but you must treat it this way and earn it.

Treat it like it is one of the most important, life-changing things in your life because it is. It will change your life, if you take it seriously. It works if you do.

How do you know if you are taking your business seriously enough? Are you doing all the previous 6 steps mentioned here? If not, then you are not taking your business seriously.

Business is a marathon and not a sprint. It is not something you just 'try out' for six months and see if it works for you. These habits are a life choice.

Building Your Franchise

You Only Ever Need 4 Good People

It's common for brand new people to think that they need to get hundreds of people to build a successful business.

The truth is that you can build a really successful organisation of over 100,000 people, and be making £10K per month, and all you ever did was build a team of 4 good people.

Does this surprise you?

This is because of the power of "Compounding," which Einstein called the 8th wonder of the world, and is also what makes network marketing so great a business to own.

Your primary goal when first starting out is to build a power team of 4 good people, who then in turn, repeat the process. Your business will then begin to grow like this.

4

16

64

256

1024

As you can see, over time, your business will have over 1000 people, but all you have personally done is built and worked with a team of 4.

The great news is that for most people, having a network of over 1000 people is all you ever need to become financially independent. This is also known as having 1000 true fans.

Just in the UK alone, there are over 60,000,000 people. Let's say, for example, that just 1% of those people are actually looking for what you have.

1% of people would love to have a business and use high quality products.

This means there are 60,000 potential business partners

just waiting for you to connect with them, and remember, all you need is a power team of 4.

The great news is that with the rise of the Internet, there has never been an easier time in all of history to be able to do this. All you have to do is to realise this, get to work, and make it happen.

Reaching the Magic Point

When you first start your own business, you may be surprised with how time consuming it is. It can feel as though you have taken a step backwards.

However, when you reach the "Magic Point," everything suddenly becomes a lot easier and a lot more enjoyable.

What is the magic point?

The magic point is the point where your business begins building itself, without needing you to be there. This is when you have your primary team, and you have helped your team build their own teams.

It is a very exciting time, which is going to require some serious effort and dedication to get to, but when it happens you can suddenly get 40 hours a week back and can go full time.

How do you get to the magic point?

Once you have your power team of 4 in place, and you have helped your team do the same, you will then have a total network of 16 people.

Then, once you have helped your team off with their teams, your total network would be at 64 people. This is the magic point.

From this point on, you have 64 people in your organisation who you are not directly working with, all building their own businesses, and that you will forever be getting paid on.

Here Are The Numbers

Unfortunately, it would be amazing if we found our power team straight away, but the reality is that you may have to sponsor 5 people to find 1 good person.

This means, you will likely have to sponsor 20 people, to find your superstars.

Now you may think this might be difficult, but remember, there are 60,000 people in the UK alone that are looking for you right now.

Once you learn how to get good at sales and marketing, you will have hundreds of people to choose from.

Also, there are more people coming into this country than are being sponsored. You have an ever-expanding market.

Does this excite you? It should.

The 3 Stages of a Network Marketing Business

It is really important to learn that there are three distinct phases when building a network marketing business (in fact any business). This is going to help prepare you when first starting out.

Stage 1: The Money Isn't Worth The Time

Stage 1 is where the hours you are putting in are not worth the money you are getting paid. For most people, this will likely be year one of your business.

This is where all the learning and hard work is. It is where 20 years of the wrong habits are revealed to you, that will need to be fixed.

It can be a bitter pill to swallow because you will likely have lots of bad habits which need changing, you likely have a very low level of skill and you will probably not be very good at many aspects of the business.

Unfortunately, this is where 95% of people quit. In fact, the number one reason why people do not succeed in business is because they simply give up way to early.

As we are conditioned as "employees," we are not used to working without getting paid, and the pain of it becomes too much.

The ironic thing is that one of the main reasons people start a business in the first place is because they no longer wanted to "sell time for money" and then when they no longer get paid on the hours they work, they end up quitting.

Getting through stage one is very simple.

Treat it as you would any other profession or skill, where year one is about training and don't quit.

"If you get into business solely to make money, you won't. If you try to make a real difference, you'll find success".
Richard Branson

Don't "expect" lots of money. The fact that you can become financially independent in your first year is incredible. We will plan for this, but realise, for most this doesn't happen.

Stage 2: The Money and Time Are About Equal

Stage 2 is where the hours you are putting into your business are pretty much equal to the money you are now being paid.

For most people, this will be year two of the business.

This is a great place to be as all the hours you have put in so far are now paying off, and everything begins to compound.

All the knowledge you have learned begins to compound, all the skills you have developed begin to compound, your paychecks begin to compound and your business begins to compound.

You are now getting less rejection and more people saying yes. Talking with people and presenting to people is now much easier, far less scary, and you are really starting to enjoy it, and your belief is now growing strong.

This is a great place to be.

Stage 3: The Money Far Outweighs The Time

Stage 3 is the final stage of your business, where you are now getting paid far more money, compared to the time you are putting in.

For most people, this will be from year three onwards.

It is a sad fact that most people never this point because they quit before they had a chance to get good.

What You Need To Know About Leadership

To build an incredibly successful network marketing business, you are not only going to have to become a leader yourself, you are also going to need to learn how to develop great leaders.

So how do you build a great team of leaders that will build you a great business and work independently from you?

It starts and ends with you. You must become that great leader first.

A leadership law to remember is that you can only teach people what you have done yourself.

It is you that has to decide that you are going to do this until it works, not just try it out.

You have to be willing to learn the skills, and learn how to manage your own inner voice before anyone else does.

You have to be willing to ride the exponential income

curve first, even though you may not be seeing any money. You must lead by example.

This is what great leadership is all about.

Here is how you build a team of 4 superstars.

You are the franchise. People will be duplicating you. People will do what you do, not what you say. There are no shortcuts to this.

Do you have your vision, and why, printed out on your wall?

Do you attend all the trainings?

Do you spend 1-2 hours a day on personal development?

Do you present to 10-20 people each month?

Do you take your business very seriously?

You set the standard for your business. Your business is a reflection of you. You set the bar for your entire organisation.

You are the franchise that gets repeated over and over again. The question is, what is it repeated? People don't buy into this business, people join you.

As the late great Jim Roan said, "For things to change in your life, <u>you</u> have to change. For things to get better, <u>you</u> have to get better."

Here is the ultimate question – if you were a brand new

consultant and you could pick anyone to be sponsored by, would you pick you?

If not, why wouldn't you? Write the answers down, then get to work and fix it.

Let's drill into this a little bit deeper as it is really important and is going to show you what you need to do to completely change your results.

The Leadership Mirror

If you want great people … you have to be great.

If you want hard working people … you have to work hard.

If you want your team to have a great attitude all the time … you have to have a great attitude all the time.

Now, even if at this point, you are a team of one … perfect. Because it all starts with you.

The Universal Maxim

A great exercise to imagine is, what your business would be like if everyone in it were just like you?

What would it be like if it consisted of 1000 people, who were exactly the same as you?

> *Would it be 1000 people who are driven?*
>
> *1000 people who are hardworking?*
>
> *1000 people who never make excuses and take full responsibility for their outcomes?*
>
> *1000 people doing daily personal development?*

1000 people presenting to 10-20 people every month?

1000 people with a bulletproof follow up system?

1000 people who have a fantastic attitude?

1000 people who attend all trainings?

or (brace yourself)

Would it be, 1000 people who don't really do many presentations at all?

1000 people who all read sometimes, but life often gets in the way?

1000 people who don't really follow up?

1000 people who are not in control of their own thoughts?

1000 people who sometimes work hard but sometimes not?

1000 people who attend some trainings and but often miss them?

1000 people who make excuses and blame people and things for their outcomes?

This exercise is brutal and incredibly valuable, as it instantly shows you what you need to fix to get your business working like a dream machine.

All Great Leaders Have A Vision

In an earlier chapter, you learned how to create your vision. Which is the ultimate destination where you are going and what you are going to make happen.

Great leaders are all visionaries, which basically just means they hold this crystal clear vision in their minds. In fact, it is so clear that when they speak to people, they can paint their vision out to them vividly.

You see, in the early days before you have a team, all you have is your vision. If you don't see your vision, how is anyone else going to see it?

In summary, to become a great leader, we must lead by example and have a crystal clear vision of where we are going.

The good news is that great leaders are made, they are not born.

What You Need To Know About Marketing

If you would like to learn how to consistently have new people to present to, then you need to get better at the skill set known as "Marketing."

***"The difference between mediocrity and making millions has more to do with marketing, than any other single
business factor."*** *Jay Abraham*

Let us begin with what marketing is. Marketing is all the communications or "messages" that your business is giving out. So, as you can imagine, it's quite important.

These include:

> **Who you are**
>
> **What you do**
>
> **Why you are even in business?**
>
> **Why should people buy from you?**
>
> **What makes you different?**

It also includes, how you let the world know that you and your business even exist.

Let's start with the main objective in marketing.

The Marketing Objective

Marketing can be broken down into 3 parts:

Step 1: To identity, connect with, and attract the best quality and quantity of desirable prospects

Step 2: To convert these prospects into first time buyers

Step 3: To turn these people into lifetime clients.

Your Target Market

<u>Every single business</u> in the world has a "Target Market." To think otherwise means you may be wasting 80% of your time speaking with the wrong people.

Depending on what product or service you sell, depends on who your target market is going to be.

Speaking to everyone with a pulse is like playing darts with no dartboard.

When you know who your ideal target market is, you will then be are playing the game to a much higher standard.

What makes up your target market? In consists of:

- The best age group
- The best gender
- The best income level
- The best education level
- Their interests and passions

Let's say you have defined your target audience as:

Women 30-50 years old

Who earn £30K + per year

Educated to a degree level

Now ask yourself this, where do these people all hangout?

What meet up groups do these people go to?

What events will they be attending?

Bingo. Now you are fishing where the whales are. And remember, it is not just about the person you are actually talking to. What close network of people do you think this person has?

That's right, a close network of your ideal target market.

Now we are getting somewhere. This step alone is a massive step to you becoming a much more effective marketer.

The only thing is, there are still people in this demographic that are completely happy with their lives and are not looking to change.

So once you know the demographic, the other important element that you are looking for is, "A Burning Need."

The best people to find and work with are the ones that have a <u>burning reason why</u> they need this business.

Now, this can be any number of reasons, like needing more money, more free time with the family, better work, a purpose in life, new friends or just financial freedom.

It is your job to match the benefits of your company to this person's burning need, and show them that this might be the solution to their problems.

That's effective marketing.

Now you know who you are looking for, it is time to find out where they are in the buying cycle.

The Buying Cycle

Did you know that before anyone buys anything, they go through a "Buying Cycle"?

A series of four stages, where they go from being completely unaware they even have a problem, to first realising they do have a problem, to looking at potential solutions, and then finally buying.

This one principle alone has put tens of thousands of pounds into my pocket, and literally made millions of pounds for the businesses I previously worked with.

This information is priceless if you understand it, and then utilize it properly.

Stage 1: The person with no need or want

The first stage of the buying cycle is when a person does not even know they have a problem and so is not bothered about finding a solution.

Talking to this type of person about your business is a <u>colossal waste of time</u>. You need to be able to quickly identify whether you are talking with this type of person and if so, move on quickly.

Stage 2: The person being introduced for the first time

Now this person is similar to the person in stage 1; however, with one big difference. They actually need what you have to offer, they just don't know that this solution exists.

It is great when you are the first person to introduce your business to this type of person, but you do have to filter through a lot of unqualified people to find these people in the first place.

Stage 3: The person who knows about the business but is not yet ready to buy

The stage 3 type person is someone who has already been educated on this type of business or has already been introduced by someone else, they just are not yet 100% sure that this business is right for them.

However, 80% of the battle has already been won. These are good people to bump into.

Stage 4: The person who is ready to get started

For a short period of time, everyone will hit stage 4. This type of person knows about the business, they know they want to do it, they just need help getting started.

It can take months for people to actually get to this point, but, did you know that using the Internet, you can actually target these people with your marketing efforts? This is something that businesses could never do before, until now.

When you know where they are in the buying cycle, you can now move on to the next stage which is going fishing.

Who—> What—> How

Think of marketing like fishing. When it comes to catching the best fish, it can be broken down into three parts.

1. <u>Where</u> you go fishing

2. The <u>bait</u> you use

3. <u>How</u> you actually fish

The most important part to finding people for your business is <u>who</u> you are targeting and talking to. It is <u>where</u> you are going fishing.

To put a number on it, I would say, 70% of the importance is <u>who</u> you are targeting and speaking to.

If you are fishing in the wrong location then everything else is a waste of time. When consultants are having trouble signing people up, it is simply because they are talking to the wrong people.

In fact, 95% of the problems people have in their business is because they are simply talking to or working with the <u>wrong people</u>.

Next up, is the <u>what</u>, which is the bait you are using to get interest.

This is also known as "The Offer." What is it you are offering people?

What is it that you actually sell?

If your answer is a business or products then, you are probably struggling and need to read the next chapter on sales.

To put a figure on it, what you are actually offering people is around 20% of the importance.

Lastly, is the <u>how</u>. How are you fishing?

This will normally be the company presentation that you are showing people.

It may surprise you that this is the least important part of what it takes to build a team. This is around 10% of what will determine if people buy.

For most people, they think it is all about the presentation. Not so.

The big problem that most people make is showing the company presentation to the wrong people and spending 90% of the time telling them about how it all works.

They then wonder, why are people not signing up?

This is also why some people just seem to "Get It" and join right away, and you may think, what did I do differently? And, sometimes you give the best presentation in the world and it falls flat.

Moving on.

What Is Your USP?

Your USP, or Unique Sales Proposition, is another critical piece of the marketing puzzle, and is actually very simple.

You just need to answer this question.

Why should someone buy from you?

That's all.

If there are ten other people/companies/products that this person could choose from, why should they buy from you?

Once you nail your USP, it will be like flicking a switch, and all of a sudden you will have more people calling you about getting started.

Moving on.

The Importance of <u>Proof</u>

Once you are sitting down with the right person, around 70% of what is going to make this person buy is <u>proof</u>.

Think about it, if they knew 100% that this is going to work for them, then everyone would do it straight away, right?

So we must demonstrate that what we are talking about is possible and that other people have already done it. Meaning, they can too.

We do this by telling stories and showing testimonials and case studies from either yourself or of other people.

<u>Show them</u> that there have been other people, just like them, who have also done what they would like to do.

For example, if the person you are talking to is an accountant, show them a case study of someone in the company who used to be an accountant, and is now financially independent.

The Magic Formula

This brings us to the final part of the marketing puzzle. How to make a sale.

Here is the formula to remember:

Leads x Conversion = Sales

One of the best parts about network marketing is that 90% of the business has already been done for you.

Someone else has already created the brand, the products, the distribution, the customer services, the legal aspects, payment systems, etc.

Your job is just to master the art of marketing and sales. Otherwise known as lead generation and conversion.

Lead generation is all about building "Systems" that give you regular contact with the highest quality and quantity of desirable prospects.

Conversion is all about converting those prospects into first time buyers, and then lifetime business partners and customers.

5 Ways To Generate More Leads Than You Can Handle

Learning how to consistently generate a flow of high quality leads, is possibly the number one skill you need to learn and develop.

Leads are the lifeblood of any business, not just in network marketing, and it is probably the number one problem that most people have.

I could list 50 ways on how to generate more leads; however, I am purposely only going to include, what I believe, to be the top six ways.

It is a better strategy to get really good at a few methods of meeting new people than it is to try to do too many badly.

Just get really good at these top 6 below, and you will never run out of finding good quality people to talk to.

 ## 1. Referrals

Referrals are by far the most effective, cheapest and fastest way to grow any business, not just in network marketing. This is because you are talking with people who already know, like and trust you.

This kind of trust and relationship can take weeks and even months to build. This is why most of the top network marketing companies will start with the "100 name list" strategy.

The 100 name list is basically where you make a list of

every person that you know. This instantly gives you 100 high quality leads, which you can begin to get started with.

Remember this: If you do this one marketing channel well, you will never need another way of generating leads. As you can build a strong business through referrals alone.

 ## 2. Online Marketing

The Internet has changed the way in which the world is now doing business. For the first time in history, you can target people who are already interested and looking to start in network marketing.

Online marketing can be broken down further into sub-channels including blogging, paid advertising, social media, video marketing, PR, direct response and email marketing.

Online marketing is not the fastest way to generate regular leads, which means it is not the easiest to duplicate; however, once up and running it is very effective.

Note: You could theoretically stop here. With just those two marketing strategies, there are more leads than you will ever need.

 ## 3. Events

Events are a great way to meet like-minded people. You can choose events which you are not only interested in yourself, but also have a high number of your target audience.

By attending an event, you are instantly surrounded by hundreds of high quality prospects. You just need to develop the skill set of being able to connect with people and create interest in watching your presentation.

Events are fun to attend, you will also be learning while you are there, and it's an environment where it's easy to talk with people as it is more socially expectable.

Starting conversations with strangers is something that gets easier the more you do it until you get to the point where you wonder how it ever intimidated you.

Eventually, you will want to be putting on your own events as this is a great way of presenting to 10-20 people on a consistent basis.

Putting on your own event also develops you into a leader, gives you instant authority and expert status and means you can duplicate this through your entire business, helping you grow 100x faster.

4. Meet Up Groups

Meet up groups are similar to events but are just on a smaller scale. Most cities run meet up groups, where you can regularly meet new people who are interested in the same things as you.

The two main places in the UK are MeetUp.com and CitySocializer.com.

You can attend meet ups on leadership, small business, health and fitness, entrepreneurship and so on.

Start by selecting just one event or meet up that you will attend each week and get chatting with people. When you feel more comfortable, you can begin transitioning to getting contact details.

5. Everyday Opportunities

Everyday opportunities are everywhere. Most people are closed off to the world and do no realise that there are opportunities for meeting new people all the time in everyday life.

You can either directly or indirectly open conversations with people, and you will be surprised where they lead.

Again, at first this can feel very uncomfortable as most of us are brought up not to talk to strangers. However, it does become easier and more natural over time.

Abundance Vs Scarcity

It is quite common for new people to have scarcity mindsets. Which means believing that it is hard to find people or that there are just not enough people to talk with.

The truth is that there are millions of people you can connect with, you simply just do not have the right skill set yet to able to do it.

We are living in a population explosion. There are millions more people being born than ever before. There will always be more people to talk to than actually being sponsored.

You just need to learn how to make the connection. Also known as <u>marketing</u>.

ACTION STEPS

Book a strategy session with your sponsor, and create a plan that is going to give you a way of regularly meeting new people to present to. This is one of the most important parts of your business to develop.

8 Ways To Get More People Saying, Yes!

Once you have developed the skills of lead generation, which is getting people to present to, you now need to get good at turning prospects into business partners and customers.

Here are the top 8 ways to double your conversion rate, meaning getting more people saying yes.

1. Target Better People

As we have learned, the fastest way to improve your marketing and get more people saying yes, is to target and speak to <u>better quality people</u>.

People who have money.

People who want what you are offering.

People who have a burning need.

People who want to start a business.

2. Following Up

Many new people make the mistake of presenting to people and then never follow up. Following up with people you have already talked to is critical.

This is because it takes on average 7-10 exposures or touch points for people to really understand what this is, feel comfortable, and then move to the final stage of the buying cycle.

You always want to be progressing people with exposures

by giving valuable information, educational and nurturing the seed that was previously planted in the presentation.

The fact is that most people do not say yes straight away. Many of the top income earners initially said no. Developing a good follow up system is crucial.

3. Personal Development

Remember this: The better you get, the easier it all becomes. Network marketing is not hard or easy. It is what it is. What makes it hard or easy is <u>you</u> and <u>your</u> current level of skill.

Ask Tiger Woods if he finds golf hard. Obviously he does not. Through hours of practice, he has developed his skills, and it is now second nature.

The same is true with business.

Picture a set of scales, on one side is your level of skill, and on the other side, is your ability to sponsor people.

As you read books, listen to audios, attend trainings and practice, the scales begin shifting until one day, it drops, and you begin signing people up left, right and centre.

If you currently find network marketing difficult, <u>you</u> simply need to get better.

4. The Use of Proof

How much time in your presentations are you spending on demonstrating proof? Remember 70% of your marketing should be based on proof.

How can you use more proof to give you a more powerful

message? Present to people with your sponsor, showcase studies and testimonials of people just like them who have become successful.

Tell stories of people just like them who broke through what they were previously doing and became successful, and watch how this affects your interactions.

5. Selling Benefits and Not Just Features

It is not only critical that you know the difference between features and benefits, but you must make sure that you are selling the benefits of owning a business and using the products.

We will be going into depth and features and benefits in the next chapter; however, for now, just remember that people buy <u>benefits</u>.

6. Nailing Your USP

What is your USP? Why should people choose network marketing? Why should people work with you? This is not optional, defining the USP is a must in any business.

How do you know when you have a good USP? People will start choosing you and your products over anyone else or continuing to do nothing at all.

7. Diet and Exercise

It may surprise you that I have included diet and exercise as being one of the best ways to increase your conversions, but it is actually really obvious.

If you look and feel great all of the time, this is often more attractive to people than anything else. You will be giving off an entirely different energy to people that shows you have got life figured out, and they are going to want to know your secret.

On the flip side, if you are out of shape, look tired and lack energy, why would people want to know more about what you are doing and join you? When you meet people, they are looking at <u>you</u> more than what you are saying.

This is so important that we will be going into more detail later.

8. Practice Practice Practice

Champions are not made in competition. Champions are made in training.

In your first few weeks and months, you will likely be saying the wrong things, at the wrong time, to the wrong people. By practising, the better you will get at saying the right things, to the right people, at the right time.

You can only fine tune these essential micro-skills by practicing over and over again. You must practise and fail and practise again and again and again <u>until</u> you get good.

One of your first goals as a new consultant should be to get to 100 presentations as soon as you can. This is the fastest way to get the results you want.

There are many more ways in which to improve your conversion rate and get more people saying yes, but these are the most important.

Again, it is better to get good at a few things than to be average at many. I only included these specific ones for a good reason.

You now know how to find people to talk to and get people to say yes, which is about 10% of the importance. The 90% is going out and doing it.

Do You Know Your Numbers

If you have a business, you need to know your key numbers. These are also known as KPIs (key performance indicators).

This includes how many people you are presenting to each month, your conversion rate, sales and profits.

In network marketing, the average conversion rate is 1:10. Meaning, for every presentation you do, roughly 1 in 10 people will join your business in some way.

A lesser known statistic is that on average, only 1 in 5 people will actually stick and become one of your power team.

This means that 4 out of 5 people on average, are going to quit (unless they read this book of course).

This is not good or bad, it is just the way it is.

This also means that you will likely have to sponsor around 20 people to find your power team of 4.

These are the facts of network marketing. The smart marketer understands these and cracks on. Remember, in the UK alone there are 60,000,000 people.

How Do I Know When I'm Good At Marketing?

I will end this chapter by saying, you will know when you are getting good at marketing when you will be getting more enquires and people showing interest than you are able to work with. It is a great problem to have.

Remember, the good news is that great network marketers are made and not born. These are all learnable skills, and every master was once a disaster.

What You Need To Know About Sales

This brings us nicely on to… sales. Another completely misunderstood part of business by most people.

If you would like to discover how to get more people saying, yes to your business opportunity, then you are going to love this chapter.

Now I personally <u>love</u> this subject. I think this is because (like network marketing) sales is another one of the most misunderstood subjects out there.

I am looking forward to setting things straight and changing how you think about sales forever.

Ready?

Now, what people do not realise is that sales is everywhere. In nearly every conversation, every time you turn on your TV, open your computer, look in a magazine, walk down the street, go to a job interview, attend a meeting, talk with your child, and on and on and on.

The smart person realises that <u>everyone is already in sales</u>. You can either realise this and use it to your advantage, or forever be on the receiving end.

What comes to your mind when I say the word, <u>sales</u>?

If you are like most people I talk to, then maybe the image of a slick guy in a suit, talking the talk and maybe someone trying to sell you something that you don't particularly want or need, may come to mind.

So let's just set this straight. This is not what sales are about.

That was an example of "Bad Sales." So, what most people "think" is sales, is actually an example of bad sales. I actually hate this about sales too.

The first step to becoming good in sales is to wipe out any thought in your head that sales are a bad thing.

Now, the word "Sell" is an Old English word meaning "to give or serve." So remember this: Good sales is all about "Service."

As we learned in an earlier chapter, business is about making people's lives better in some way, and the "sale" is just the final part of the process.

What Is A Sale?

A sale will happen when a person genuinely believes that they will become better off after the transaction. That's it.

So your job, as a salesperson, is to make that person's life better off. It is to help the person you are talking to solve their problem, fill their need, or reach their goal. Please read that again.

Good sales are all about the other person. Their wants, their needs, their dreams, their goals, their frustrations, their sticking points. Your job is to help them.

Example of a Perfect Sale

One day, you wake up and discover you have a problem and need to go and see the doctor. After arriving at the surgery, you sit and wait until the doctor is free.

When you are called in, you then sit with the doctor as he asks you questions until he knows exactly what the problem is that you have.

He then explains to you what your problem is, why you have it, and what you need to do to fix it.

He then sends you on your way with a prescription to purchase, and you feel you have been taken care off. Problem solved.

What a great sales person that doctor was. You didn't even know you had been sold to, but you were. Good sales are an invisible process.

Example of a Bad Sale

One day, you wake up and are having a great morning when, all of a sudden, a friend calls you up and asks to meet you but does not say why. She was a bit weird on the phone and made you feel a little bit uncomfortable.

You agree, and later that day you are sitting with your friend having coffee. All of a sudden your friend launches into an amazing business opportunity, and you are asked to buy something.

You feel completely 'sold to' and feel your friend doesn't really care about what is going on in your life right now, they are only thinking about their own needs.

See the difference? This is not good sales.

The Inner Game of Sales and Wealth

Before we start with the specific techniques and strategies, we need to take a look at what is happening below the water.

The actual words you use with people are just the tip of the iceberg. You communicate far more through your body language and your beliefs which is why these need fixing first.

This is important because until we fix the inner game of sales, the outer game of what to say will not work for you.

What is the inner game of sales?

These are all your thoughts and beliefs about money, business, sales and you, that you have learned over your life by your experiences, and the people you have been around.

For example, if you believe that you probably aren't going to become successful … then, I am sorry to say, you are probably not going to become successful.

However, if you hold the belief that it is only a matter of time until you are successful, then this is also what will likely become your reality.

This sounds very simple and it is. It is also very powerful, so take this seriously. We have to fix your beliefs.

Now, your beliefs have been learned over decades of conditioning from parents, friends, teachers and society.

The beliefs you are currently "holding onto," are giving you everything you have in life right now.

If you want different fruits in your life then we are going to need to change the roots.

The Power of Beliefs?

Imagine you are going on a journey. You are driving in your car, and you have started on your way.

Now, there are two types of beliefs.

The first kind is called "Limiting Beliefs." These are the beliefs that you currently have that are not helping you at all with the new goals that you have.

A visual example of these beliefs would be like having the breaks applied in your car. It is slowing you down and making your journey a lot harder.

The second kind of beliefs is called "Empowering Beliefs." These are the beliefs you have which really help you with your goals and make everything easier.

The visual example would be like having a new engine put in your car making you go twice as fast.

Let us now look at the core beliefs that all of the <u>most successful network marketers</u> in the world have.

I am not just saying this. All the top earners 100% genuinely believe what I am about to share with you.

Belief 1. There Has Never Been A Better Time In History To Be Involved in Network Marketing

Now this is easy to say, but do you truly believe it?

Having a job is great in the short term as you work a month and then get paid. This is great. However, in the medium to long term, jobs are terrible.

Why is this?

It is because, with a job, you can never stop working for the rest of your life. Because if you do, your income stops. Also, with a job you are on track to retire on the equivalent of minimum wage.

Now, as far businesses and investments go, there is nothing else out there that compares to the return you get with a network marketing business.

With very little money in, you can build a business that can generate tens of thousands of pounds a month, that eventually, does not require you to be there.

There is nothing else out there that even comes close to this. And, with the rise of the Internet and being able to connect with hundreds of people, there has never been a better time.

Belief 2. This is Absolutely, The Best Company To Be With

You must believe to your very core that the company you are with is the very best option. That they have fantastic products that actually benefit the lives of each person who uses them.

That it is the right timing, in the right market, with the right payment plan and you are with the right people. You have everything you need from a business point of view.

Belief 3. Wealth Requires Work

We all want the easy path to wealth and success, I know I did. What I learned over the years of jumping from one 'push button system' or easy claim to money to another, is that wealth requires work.

This is obvious if you think about it. If anyone could become wealthy within one year, without any serious effort then everyone would be wealthy, but, they are not. Only 1 in 10 people is.

Wealth requires work.

The hard path is actually working 40 hours a week until you retire, on the equivalent of minimum wage at age 67.

The easy way is to work hard for 3-5 years with your own business and retire rich.

The only faster way than this is either the national lottery or by inheritance. All the top earners know this, and they know that you are going to have to do things for a few years that most people are not prepared to do.

Belief 4. I Have Access To Everything I Need to Become Successful

The best part about network marketing is that it does not matter about your age, gender, background, religion, education level or upbringing, etc., there are people who have started from worse positions than you are in right now, who have become successful.

You have access, right now, to all the books, audios, trainings and support that you will ever need. You just need to realise this and take action.

Belief 5. Even If I Don't Earn A Single Penny in My First Year, I Can Still Become Successful

A big mistake people fall into is comparing themselves with the 5%. You see, 1 in 20 people do make money very quickly in network marketing.

Although this is fantastic and achievable for everyone, for most people, the reality is that the first year will require a lot of learning, personal development and trial and error before you begin to breakthrough.

Even if you don't earn a single penny in your first year, you can still become very successful.

The Psychology of People

When building any kind of business, there is one thing that is certain. You are going to have to work with and communicate with people.

This makes it really important to know how people think.

Now that you know that there has never been a better time in history to be building a network marketing business, you know you are with the best company, with the best products and with the best people, it is time to learn about the most important factor in a sale … the other person.

We must STOP for a second and realise what is going on in all of our heads all the time. We spend 95% of every day wrapped up in our own problems and issues.

We are constantly thinking about our needs and wants, problems and work life, goals and money situation and relationship challenges and so on.

We all want to be richer, healthier, happier, have an amazing partner, have close friends and intimate relationships, enjoy good food, go to amazing places, be respected, get more recognition and be appreciated.

Why am I telling you this?

Because, your job as a salesperson is to <u>get out of your head</u> and into the head of the other person.

In business and in sales, it is all about <u>them</u>. Everything you say should be to benefit the person you are speaking with. Everything you do should benefit that person in some way.

Sales = Service.

This is the shift you need to make that will take you from forever struggling, to signing people up left right and centre.

You need to know their wants, their needs, their goals, their dreams and what their aspirations are. Once you know this, you can then be the one to help them and provide the solution.

The biggest mistake people make in sales is offering the solution before uncovering their problem or need.

Let me drill this home. It is NOT about you. People do not care that you have a business. People do not care that you need to hit your goal.

If it comes across in any way that this interaction is benefitting you in any way, then NO SALE.

One last point. When I say about saying things that demonstrate you care about them and their problems. What you have to do is ACTUALLY care about them and solving their problems.

We Don't Want 9 Out Of 10 People

Sales is first and foremost a disqualification process.

Not everyone wants or needs what you have to offer. Also, you do not want most people in your business. You are looking for a very specific type of person.

Most people will waste your valuable time and energy. You are choosing the right person for your business just as much as they are choosing you.

This means we must first define what it is we are looking for. We then need a way of quickly disqualifying people and being able to sort the good from the bad.

The 4 Qualifiers

1. Does this person have the money to start a business?
2. Does this person have a burning reason why?
3. Is this person serious about becoming successful?
4. Do you want this person as a business partner?

When you are speaking with people, you need to find out as quickly as possible if they fit your criteria because if they don't, you are wasting your precious time speaking to the wrong person.

Only 1 in 20 people is actually right for this business. Only 1 in 20 people has a real desire to improve their life. Only 1 in 20 people will actually do what is required. Only 1 in 20 people have a good work ethic.

<u>You</u> only want 1 in 20 people for your business.

You don't want everyone with a pulse. This is a trap that new people fall into out of desperation to sign their first person.

You will get better at disqualifying over time and with practice. Remember, you have standards. You have an amazing gift for the right person.

Who Is Controlling The Frame?

We now move into actual conversations.

In every single conversation, there is a "Frame" that one person is controlling.

What is a frame?

The frame is the "Meaning of the Conversation." If you get the meaning of the conversation right, then you really can't say the wrong thing. The words you are actually saying are just the tip of the iceberg.

The meaning of the conversation should be that you are here to help them. You are talking with them because they have a problem, and you have the solution.

If the meaning of the conversation ever becomes about you being there to somehow make money from them or to just make a sale, then nothing you say will work.

If people ever _feel_ they are being sold to in any way, then you have messed up.

You must enter the conversation demonstrating that you are in full control of your life, and they are the ones that are currently stuck. You have got it all figured out, and they want to know how to fix it.

Who is chasing who?

As you are speaking with people, be aware who is chasing who. This is the frame. This is all the communication going on behind the actual words.

If you find that you are chasing them, and you are the one calling them and leaving voice mail messages for them to get back to you, then this is a sign that you have been doing something wrong.

You are communicating that you need them. And that you are chasing them. And that you have the problem and they are the solution. This is very subtle communication, but it makes the difference from sponsoring to struggling.

When you begin to get good at sales, you will notice that they will be the ones chasing you, they will be the ones calling you and leaving messages for you to get back to.

You are the prize. People need what _you_ have. The frame must always be that they are the ones with the problem and you have the solution. People should be grateful that you are sharing your precious time with them and not vice versa.

Salesmanship is an "Art Form" that needs to be studied, practiced and developed over time.

Know What You Are Selling

Through understanding what business is and developing strong marketing, we now find ourselves talking with a good quality prospective client.

We have mentally asked our 4 qualifying questions and uncovered their needs and goals, it is now time to begin educating this person on a possible solution, meaning your business.

This is when we make our presentation and begin talking about the business and the products and is another landmine that beginners mess up.

My question to you is this, what are you selling?

If you think you are selling a business, or skin care or nutrition or utilities or coffee or whatever your company's product line is, you are wrong, and I will make a guess that you are struggling.

Now, when it comes to the actual products, you <u>must</u> know the difference between a feature and a benefit.

Features and Benefits?

The simple way to explain the difference between a feature and a benefit is that a feature is something about what the product or service <u>is,</u> and a benefit is something about what the product or service will <u>do</u> for them.

Example.

You might say to someone, "Have you ever thought about starting a business?" A business is a feature or part of what you offer.

What is more important is what a business can do for that person.

A business is a way that you can double your income. Being able to double your income is a benefit.

Another example.

This protein is "Vegan Approved." Vegan approved is a feature.

Which means that because it is dairy free, it isn't going to leave you bloated and gassy as other protein shakes do. Easy digestion and saving on any embarrassment is the benefit.

Make sense?

The reason this is so important is because it has been proven that <u>people buy benefits,</u> they do not buy features.

Or said another way, people will buy what the product will do for them, not what the product is.

If you are just talking about features all the time and stopping there, then I can tell you now, many people are probably not buying from you.

Let me drill this home a little deeper.

People <u>do not</u> want to start a business!

People <u>do not</u> want your products!

They do want what a business or the products will do for them. People do want to make more money and have more free time with the family.

People do want to look younger, have more energy every day, to live longer and get comments from their friends.

This is what you are selling.

People do not want a Hoover, they want a clean carpet.

People do not want sun cream, they do not want to be burnt.

People do not want a new gas supplier, they want to have more money to spend.

People do not want a business, they want a higher income.

People do not want face cream, they want to look younger.

Make sense?

So, action step, find out the top three features and benefits of your business and your companies products, and be sure you are talking to people about the benefits you offer, not just the features, and watch the difference it makes.

The Power of Stories

Wherever effective communication is involved, you will find stories. Storytelling is a powerful part of any marketer's tool kit and I am not referring to the kind of stories found in Disney movies involving castles and dragons.

What is a story?

A story is just sharing a previous experience or event that is relevant to the current situation.

Stories give what we say <u>meaning</u> and <u>value</u>. They can help you and your team stay motivated, they will help you sponsor more people, and they will help you train great people.

You must make it a habit of collecting and building up your own "Story Bank," which you can pull from when needed.

For example, if you are speaking with someone who is worried about not having enough time for a business, you could tell a story about someone in your company who was working more hours than they are right now, who went on to become successful and is now living a far better life because of it.

This story instantly defuses the objection and makes the person suddenly want to know how this was possible.

Again, stories are a crucial part of your ongoing communications with people.

Let's do another example. Let's say someone on your team has not sponsored anyone, and they are six months in. You could tell a story about someone in your company who also didn't sponsor anyone for a year, and is now one of the top earners in the company.

Obviously, do not make stories up. They must be true.

This is a much more powerful way to communicate that not sponsoring someone right away is not as important as it may seem without just saying, don't worry about it.

Through learning and practice, you too will become a great storyteller as you learn exactly when and how to use this technique. Stories are very powerful.

The Fortune is in the Follow-Up

People may "Impulse Buy" a chocolate bar at the shop, but they do not tend to impulse buy, starting a business. It is a much bigger commitment.

In most businesses, it takes on average, 7-10 "Exposures" or "Touch Points" for people to feel comfortable enough to make a buying decision.

This means that when you sit down and show someone your presentation, 9 out of 10 people won't be ready to buy there and then. This is absolutely normal.

In fact, many of the top earners in network marketing today flat out said, "No," when they were first introduced to the business.

Let's put things into perspective. You have just shown them a completely different way to live their life to what they are used to. It takes time for their brains to adjust and for the information to sink in.

So What Should I Do?

This is why it is important to create, a bulletproof "Follow Up" system.

A "system" of educating, developing, sharing, giving value and building a connection and trust with people over a set period of time.

Leading them down the buying cycle until they realise that this is the best thing that they could be doing with their time and money right now.

How Do I Do This?

You should have 2-3 pieces of reading material and 2-3 audios that you can easily give people access to at the appropriate time.

I like to give people <u>one</u> thing to read and <u>one</u> thing to listen to at a time.

Note, you are not selling them anything. All you are doing is giving them a valuable piece of training that is improving their life in some way, and by doing so, reminding them that you can help them.

This is known as "Pull Marketing."

Remember, it's all about them, so ask yourself, what does this person need right now?

Do they need educating on whether network marketing is worth doing? Or, do they need educating on why your company is the right one to choose, and so on?

> **Remember:** Most people do not join right away and that an important part of business is in the follow up.

What does your current follow-up system look like?

Note: You will know when you are getting good at sales, when people are calling and chasing <u>you</u> to get started.

The good news is that sales is a learnable skill, and great salespeople are made, not born.

How To Handle Objections and FAQ's

Once you have presented the opportunity to people, it is normal for people to then have questions and/or concerns about starting a business.

In most businesses, there are only a handful of questions people ask over and over again, so you only need to get good at answering these frequently asked questions.

Here are the most frequently asked questions and the appropriate response to each. This will give you the confidence to know that you can handle most situations with ease.

"Will This Work For Me?/Could I Do It?"

As, this question is normally thought and not spoken, I like to bring it up in the presentation and use some kind of story to help them understand that there have been people in worse situations than them who have become successful and that there are thousands of people to talk with.

"I Don't Have The Money?"

Empathise, if you thought the same thing at first, tell them about it.

"Exactly, does not having any money not annoy you? The fact that you have worked all your life so far, and you still don't have any excess money. Would you like to have lots of excess money? Great, I can show you how. Have you any other questions?"

(If they <u>really</u> do not have £100 per month, then this business isn't for them right now. They need to fix their current situation first before starting a business. Help them.)

"I Don't Have The Time?"

Empathise, if you thought the same thing at first, tell them about it.

"Exactly! Does that not annoy you? The fact that you have worked all your life so far and you still do not have any free time to do all the things you want to do? Would you like to have lots of free time?

"I can show you how to get 40 hours per week from your full time job back and never have to work 40 hours a week ever again. Have you any other questions?"

"Isn't This Illegal or a Pyramid Scheme Thing?"

This actually doesn't come up very often at all.

"No, this is a common misconception. Pyramid schemes are illegal. This company has been around [x] number of years and turns over [x] number of pounds. Have you ever thought about owning your own business?"

"I'm Not Very Good At Sales"

Empathise, if you thought the same thing at first, tell them about it.

"This really isn't about selling products. It is more about educating people that there is a much smarter way to make a living, that thousands of people are now deciding to do.

"It's basically just doing what we are doing now. The best people are teachers more than sales people."

"I Need To Do Some Research, I'll Think About It"

Empathise, if you thought the same thing at first, tell them about it.

"Yes I agree. This can be a lot to take in at first. Have you got any other questions at this point?"

Just be sure to give them some follow-up material as standard.

"It's Got A Bad Reputation"

Empathise, if you thought the same thing at first, tell them about it.

"Here is the interesting thing. Have you noticed that many top business leaders like Donald Trump and Robert Kiyosaki, all say network marketing is a great thing to do, yet there are some people who disagree and say the opposite?

It comes down to the 90% and 10%. 90% of people do not have any business experience, are living paycheck to paycheck and are the ones who will tell you that this may not be a good thing to do.

"And it is the 10% of people who are <u>business owners</u>, have lots of money that tell you it's the right thing to do. You need to decide who you are going to listen to."

"What Is The Training Like?"

"The training is excellent. You will be given access to a two thousand pound training program.

"You will also be getting training calls every couple of days from myself, where I teach you our simple system for success, and there are training sessions every month in your area, where other people from the company get together and you get to learn from top experts and meet other like-minded people."

(This is obviously company specific.)

"What Are The Next Steps/How Do I get Started?"

Getting started is really simple. You simply register an account on the main website and order your first month's worth of products. I will then send you the "getting started guide," which will talk you through everything that you need in the first month.

We will then have our training calls every couple of days for the first week or two so I can teach you with everything you need to know on how to become successful.

The next step is to set a time where I help you get registered and then as soon as the registration goes through we can start your training. Is there anything else you need to know from me before we start?

(This is also company specific.)

PART 3:

Turning Pro

A very common thought that people have, especially in their first few months is," Is this going to work for me?"

The truth is that the only person who decides whether this business is going to work for you or not, is <u>you</u>.

It really is that simple.

One of the biggest secrets to success in business is being prepared to do things that most people are not prepared to do. This is not rocket science. It is just the case of treating this as a profession and training <u>until</u> you get good.

All the people who give up just didn't take their business seriously. They did not treat it as the life-changing vehicle that it is.

Network marketing works if you do. No one is going to give you a business that generates £10,000 per month, with free holidays and cars. You are going to have to <u>earn it</u>. You have to fight for it.

You have to put in your 10,000 hours. No matter what business, career, skill or profession you choose to go into, this holds true.

Forget "Get Rich Quick."

It's time to get serious. It's time to take your business serious. It's time to take learning about sales, marketing and leadership serious.

Now, if you are reading this right now, it means you are in the top 10% of people who are prepared to educate themselves and get good, so just know that you are on the right track.

I am here to tell you, you have what it takes. You are worthy. There are people who have started in worse situations than you who have done it, and so can you.

But, business is harder than just having a job, where all you have to do is turn up. You are going to have to put in the hours as with anything worthwhile.

Blocking Out All The Noise

With the rise of the Internet giving everyone a voice, there is now so much noise out there, and it is only going to get worse.

What do I mean by noise?

It is all the opinions, remarks, articles, blogs, little comments, negative people and people who have tried network marketing for a few weeks and quit and so on.

Because only 1 in 20 people are destined to become business owners, by default, it means you are going to need to develop strong filters to block out all the rubbish that is going to come your way from 19 out of 20 people.

This means a general rule of thumb, 90% of people you talk with, read, watch or listen to on a day-to-day basis, is not good information to take in and is going to be a distraction.

You must learn how to block out all the noise. Unsubscribe from all the emails, don't even read the blog posts from all the broke employees, who, unfortunately have an opinion (and they will gladly let you know it).

Your financial future depends on this.

Just remember, top business owners, best-selling authors, and multi-millionaires including, Donald Trump, Robert Kiyosaki, T Harv Eker, Stephen Covey, Darren Hardy etc., all tell you that network marketing is one of the best things you can do.

Everyone else you meet in everyday situations, including family and friends, co-workers may tell you that this profession is to be avoided.

The question you must constantly ask yourself is this. Who are you going to listen to? It all depends on where you want to end up.

Would you take marriage advice from someone who has never been married?

Then do not take business advice from anyone who is not a business owner. The challenge with this is that it is going to be most people you meet and speak with. Prepare for it now. It is coming.

The 3 Biggest Mistakes New Network Marketers Make

If you would like to learn why most of the people fail in this business, so that you know how you can easily avoid these silly mistakes, then here they are.

Mistake 1: They Give Up Way Too Early

The sad truth is that most people simply give up way too early. Why is this? It is because people begin in business with the wrong mindset and expectations.

People have been conditioned as employees and self-employed people and to work for money. Then, if they do make money in their first year, it becomes too painful and they give up.

For most people, year one is about working your ass off and developing the business skills that are going to give you success.

You will have massive breakthroughs in year two onwards if you just stick with the training and keep at it.

Yet most people quit in their first year, which is insanity. Starting in business is no different to wanting to become a doctor, accountant, a sports professional or master any other skill.

The fact that you even have the possibility to make money in your first year is a massive bonus, which no other industry offers. Every other major industry requires at least 3 years training before you even begin working for an income.

Mistake 2: They Do Not Follow The System

For many different reasons, people simply do not follow the system that is laid out for them. Mainly due to fears, insecurity, lack of skill and frustration.

You are really going to have to work on making 7 habits for success part of your everyday life, and in a couple of years, you too will get the same results. The challenge is not letting life or excuses get in the way.

If you fall off the bike, no problem, simply get back on and try again.

Mistake 3: They Let the 90% Influence Them

As you go through your first year, you are going to come across a lot of noise of previously mentioned, including negativity and rejection mainly from employees and self-employed.

It is critical to your success to know who to listen to. Do not listen to the 90% of people who do not have what you want. Only listen to successful business owners and people who are on the same mission as you.

The good news is that this will get easier and easier over time. Until, one day, you will notice that it just doesn't even bother you anymore.

5 Steps To Managing Your Time Effectively

Time management is a skill set which you should take very seriously and take the time to get really good at.

Why is this?

Good time management skills will help make your life 100x easier, more enjoyable and will help grow your business 100x faster, so it's very important.

Having read several books and taken different courses on time management, I am now only going to include the most valuable in this chapter.

These are "habits" to condition into your daily routine, and once you have them, watch how much faster things begin to change for you.

1. Use A Monthly Planner

Begin using some kind of monthly planner. I personally like to use a free notepad that is on my computer.

This is simply a big list of everything that you need to do in this current month. This is where you list everything, including non-business tasks.

Ask yourself, what are all the things that I have to do this month that will make this a really productive month? and then list them out.

2. Use A Daily To Do List

Once you have your master list of things to do, you then should pull them from this list and add them to your daily to-do list each day.

Again, ask yourself, if I was going to make this a really productive day, what are all the things I would have to do? And again list them. 5-7 items are a good benchmark.

3. Plan Your Day The Night Before

Get into the habit of finishing your day with planning for the following day.

One of the most productive habits you can develop is to plan what you are going to do each day the night before.

10 minutes of planning, literally saves you hours of wasted time the following day as you will always be working from a highly productive list.

4. Utilise The 80:20 Principle To The Max

Most people have heard about Pareto's 80:20 principle, which says that 80% of the outcome, comes from 20% of the effort.

However, this is just the tip of the iceberg on using this principle effectively.

How are some examples of the original 80:20 rule in daily use.

80% of your current results are coming from 20% of the time you spend each day.

80% of what makes people eventually join your business, are coming from 20% of what you are actually saying to them.

80% of your current problems are coming from 20% of the tasks that need doing.

And so on.

What people do not realise is that the real power of the 80:20 principle comes from its repetition. You see, you can do an 80:20 analysis on the top 20%. This will gives us the top 4% which is where we find the real gold.

However, to harness the super power of this principle is when we do an 80:20 analysis of the top 4%. When we do this, we uncover the top 1%.

This brings us to one of the most important lessons in this entire book. What we have just uncovered is:

80% of whatever you are measuring, is coming from 20% of the effort.

64% of whatever you are measuring, is coming from just 4% of the effort.

And most importantly.

52% of whatever you are measuring, is coming from just 1% of the effort.

Said another way, by working on the most important 1%, you can improve things by over 50%.

Drill this 1% law of nature into your entire being.

By always focusing on the most important 1% of any task, it is giving you, on average 52% of the end result.

This is the key to constantly being incredibly effective. It means you will always be getting the maximum result from the minimum amount of effort and time being put in.

Let's put this into practice. This means:

By working on the most important 1% of all the tasks you could be doing, it will give you 52% of your results.

By finding out what is the most important 1% of what you are saying to people, it will give you 52% of the impact that ultimately makes people join.

And finding out what the number one sticking point is that you currently have and fixing it will grow your business by over 50%.

Over half of the damage that your negative self talk is doing right now is only coming from <u>one thing</u> you are saying to yourself. Replace it with a positive affirmation right now.

You always want to be asking yourself what is the one thing I should be working on right now?

5. Put A Value On Your Time

Now we know the importance of working on the most important tasks, what are the most important tasks?

Here is a breakdown of all the main tasks you are spending time on right now.

I have put them into "Hourly Income" columns of:

£10 per hour tasks,
£100 per hour tasks,
£1000 per hour tasks,
£10,000 per hour tasks.

So you can instantly see where you should be spending your time. This chart will provide new perspective and insights and change your business.

£10 per hour	£100 per hour	£1000 per hour	£10,000 per hour
Your 9-5 job	Talking to a qualified prospect	Planning and prioritising your day	Improving your vision, why, usp and story
Talking to unqualified prospects	Exercise	Presenting the opportunity	Public speaking and doing workshops
Cold calling (of any variety)	Following up	Personal development	Executing brilliant ideas
Cleaning, sorting	Outsourcing tasks	Running new marketing campaigns	
Running errands	Training your team	Attending training events	
Worrying, complaining	Creating marketing campaigns to test	Working on the top 1% of any critical task	
	Tracking KPI's	Goal setting	

The Business Athlete Training System

In today's culture, we are being asked to work harder and harder, which forces people into bad habits like missing sleep, eating fast food and not getting enough (if any) exercise, all of which leads to low energy, fatigue and eventually burn out.

How important is health and fitness to productivity?

Only Ever 24 Hours Away From Animals

Simply do not eat, drink or sleep for 24 hours and see how productive you are. The reality is that we are always only 24 hours from being animals.

When we begin skipping these vital components, our work deteriorates very quickly.

> **Our Objective:** To build the capacity to sustain high performance in the face of increasing demand. The business athlete training system is split into four categories.

We obviously do not have time to go into a full program of health and fitness.

Just note that if you do not regularly feel great and full of energy, then you have slipped into bad habits which can easily be corrected to get you back on track.

Feeling great and energised is our natural state. Get these 4 key areas right and you will look and feel a lot healthier and be a lot more productive.

The following tips may sound too simple but really make sure you check to see if you are doing each one.

Key Area 1: Hydration

Dehydration causes you to have poor concentration, feel tired and lethargic. Check that you are drinking water regularly to stay hydrated, full of energy and feeling great.

Many times when you are feeling tired, it is because you have simply not drunk enough water, not due of lack of sleep which it can feel like.

ACTION STEPS

→ Drink a glass of water as soon as you wake up
→ Drink 6-8 glasses of water daily

Key Area 2: Exercise

We are built to move, not sit. If you do not brush your teeth each day, they will begin to deteriorate. If you do not eat, then your body begins to deteriorate.

The same is true for exercise. If you do not exercise each day, then your body begins to get fat, weak and problems arise.

A 30-60 minute daily exercise routine should be a daily habit. If you do not currently do this then you have simply got caught up in life, and it now needs fixing.

Anyone can exercise for 30 minutes in the morning, no matter what duties people have. No excuses.

This too will help you look good, feel good, give you more energy and a persona of vitality which will begin to attract people.

ACTION STEPS

→ Create a 30-60 minute daily exercise routine

Key Area 3: Rest and Recovery

Unlike computers, your body needs rest. You may have heard many times about getting 8 hours sleep each night; however, do you actually get 8 hours? If not, how can you fix this? It is time to get serious.

Research on our ability to focus has proven that when we do work, working in 60-90 minute intervals will help you get twice as much done while being able to work less.

After working for over 2 hours straight, your attention and productivity drop dramatically and you are actually getting less done that if you were to take a break.

It is a case of taking regular breaks and prioritising tasks, and then giving them full attention and focus and 6-90 minutes.

ACTION STEPS

→ Be sure to get 7-9 hours sleep each night
→ Take regular breaks from work every 60-90 minutes

Key Area 4: Nutrition

If your body was a car, what would you put in it? If you fill your car with junk, it is not going to run for very long and you will soon begin to get problems. The same is true for your body.

You will have probably heard, you are what you eat. Now is the time to stop hearing the phrase and actually do something about it.

ACTION STEPS

→ Eat 4-6 smaller meals throughout the day to maintain
high energy
→ Be sure to eat breakfast everyday
→ Eat a balanced healthy diet
→ Minimise sugar and stimulants

Are You An Amateur or Professional?

There is going to be a time in your life, when you are going to have to "Turn Pro". What is turning pro?

It is that time in your life, when you finally decide to get serious about your business and your life.

There is a wash of amateurs everywhere. People who say they want a business, try a few things out for a short period of time and then expect their business to be making thousands of pounds.

This industry does not need any more people in their first year, trying out network marketing, hoping to get rich.

What this industry is crying out for, are <u>professionals</u>. People who are ready to do what it takes, to build a business that generates significant money each month and gives them the lifestyle most people will only ever dream about.

Now, you are either one or the other. You cannot be both. There is no in-between. Which side of the fence are you going to be on? It may sound simple but this is just a decision. The decision is yours.

The Amateur

- Gives it less than a year
- Blames, Excuses, Denial
- Are The 90% or Masses
- Do Not Study Their Craft
- Hold Limiting Beliefs
- Make Your Life 10x harder

- Focus Only On Money
- See the Monthly Cost As an Expense
- Do Not Attend Trainings
- Have a Scarcity Mindset
- Thinks in Problems
- Lets Fear Stop Them
- Their Thoughts Control Them

The Professional

- The Mindset of 'Do It Until'
- Accountability, Ownership, Responsibility
- Are In Or Will Be In The Top 10%
- Trains Everyday
- Build Empowering Beliefs
- Make Your Life 10x Easier
- Focus On Skills and Delivering Value First
- Sees the Monthly Cost as an Investment
- Attends All Trainings
- Has An Abundant Mindset
- Thinks in Solutions
- Acts In-Spite of Fear
- Manages Their Thoughts
- Never Gives Up

The amateur starts a business with the mindset of "Dipping Their Toe in the Water" and seeing if it works for them or not. Most give it less than a year, some, will give it less than three months.

The professional starts a business with the mindset of "I

will do this 'until' it works." This doesn't matter if it takes a few months or a few years because they will have a great business in a few years time either way.

The amateur lives in a world of blame, excuses and denial.

The professional lives in a world of accountability, ownership and responsibility for everything they have in their life.

The amateurs are apart of the 90% of the population. The masses.

The professionals are in or will be in the top 10% of the population.

Amateurs have a get rich quick mindset and they are not prepared to study, and put in the hours required to become good at their craft.

How comfortable would you feel going to see a doctor who has not read a single book on medicine?

The professional works on their own personal development every day. Reading books, listening to audios, attending trainings and practising what they are learning.

Amateurs have picked up and hold onto "Limiting Beliefs". This can include that they might never become successful because they didn't have the right background, or education, or ability or have the right parents, etc.

Professionals work on replacing limiting beliefs with "Empowering Beliefs." They truly believe that they can find a way to become successful. They believe they are in the right industry, at the right time, with the right products and with the right people.

You will notice that amateurs make your life 10 times harder as you interact with them. You do not look forward to taking their phone calls. When you do talk with them, you find them emotionally draining. They are not fun to be around.

Professionals are great to be around and make your life 10 times easier. You really look forward to speaking with them and training with them as its fun and enjoyable.

Amateurs only focus on money. Now there is nothing wrong with wanting to make money. Most people start a business because of the financial gains they can get, I know I did.

But it can't just be about money because if money doesn't show up early on, then you will not do what it takes until it does.

Professionals love making money. They just have more reasons why they are doing this business other than money.

They know, that this type of business genuinely improves people's lives, including themselves, and they are making a positive difference in the world. They are just getting rich in the process.

Amateurs see the monthly cost of running a network marketing business as an expense and it causes them frustration each month.

Professionals see the monthly cost as an investment, and

are focusing on how to become profitable to then make that cost irrelevant.

Amateurs do not attend all the trainings put on by the companies as they would prefer to give an excuse, stay at home and watch TV.

Professionals attend all the trainings. They know that it doesn't just benefit them, it also benefits their entire organisation as they are leading by example and taking their business seriously.

Amateurs have a "Scarcity Mindset." They make excuses like, there just aren't enough people to talk with, or that everyone has heard about it already, or that the products are just too expensive, and so on.

Professionals have developed an "Abundant Mindset." They know that there are millions and millions of people to connect with.

They know they have access to all the trainings, people, resources and everything else they need to become successful. They just have to ignore all the noise and go do it.

The amateur thinks in problems. When talking with them, all you will hear is why they can't do this, and why they didn't do that.

The professional thinks in solutions. They know that there is a solution to every problem. They are aware of their problems, but they quickly ask themselves, "How do I solve this?"

Amateurs let fear stop them. We all share the same fears. Fear of failure, fear of rejection, fear of the unknown, fear of what people might think of us, even the fear of success.

The big difference is that amateurs let fear stop them, and then they make excuses as to why they didn't do what needed to be done.

Professionals have learned how to act in spite of fear. They have all the same fears, the only difference is that they fear what their life will be like if they do not take the required action. The fear of staying where they are is simply greater than what needs to be done.

Amateurs let their thoughts control <u>them</u>. We all have fears and niggles and doubts running through our heads all the time.

The difference is that amateurs let these thoughts get out of control and their thoughts control them.

The professional has learned that thoughts need managing. They know it is perfectly normal to have positive and negative thoughts; however, the difference is that the professional manages their thoughts and remains in control of them.

Amateurs give up. When things get tough, when they realise they are not making instant money, when they realise that it actually takes work to get anything of real value, they choose to give up.

Professionals have learned never to give up. They understand that 90% of people are not prepared to do the day-to-day tasks and change their bad habits.

They understand that the amateurs will come and go and that business is a marathon and not a sprint, and when you check back with them in 2 years, they are the ones that are financially free.

Are You Going To Give It 10 out of 10?

Building a business is likely going to be one of the most challenging things you have done so far; however, it is also going to be one of the most rewarding.

How many times in your life are you going to have to build a "System" that generates £10,000 per month in income?

Only <u>once</u>.

To do this, you are going to have to push yourself, and give it 10/10. Now, when you were at school, how much effort did you give it to get the grades that you got?

10 being you studied every waking hour, had early nights and gave it everything you had, and 1 being, you didn't do anything or the bare minimum?

I am guessing around 5 for effort right?

How about for your current job? On a scale of 1-10, how much effort did you give it to get where you are today? 10 being you studied day and night, read every book on the subject, interviews top experts and did every course available?

I am guessing around 7 or 8. Am I right?

When are you going to see what you can really do if you put your mind to it? When are you going to give something <u>everything</u> you have got?

This business can and will change your life, but you must treat it this way and give it all you have got. Are you ready to finally give something 10 out of 10?

We Need You

Congratulations for buying and finishing this book. It means you are serious about building a successful business, which also means that you are right on track.

I want to personally tell you to just <u>keep going</u>. We need people like you to show other people the way.

There is a mass of people struggling in life right now, and you have the vehicle to help them, but you must first push through the barriers and stick with it.

There are thousands of people who do not know this training exists, and they need you. You can do this, and when you do help other people get what they want, you will have all the things that you want and more.

I wish you happiness & success.

The 5 Best Books for Network Marketers

1. *Rich Dad Poor Dad* – Robert Kiyosaki

This is the book to get you started on the road to wealth. It was the book that was responsible for changing my life. It will show you why the rich get richer and why most people will always struggle financially.

2. *The One Thing* – Gary Keller

There is always too much to do in one day. This is the ultimate book on time management. You will learn how to use the 80:20 principle to select which things are the most important to do and be sure you are always working on the one thing.

3. *Cashflow Quadrant* – Robert Kiyosaki

The Cashflow Quadrant will show you the four ways in which people make money. Employee, Self Employed, Investor and Business Owner. You will learn how to make the critical mindset switch from employee to business owner.

4. *How To Win Friends and Influence People* – Dale Carnegie

This is one of the best books available to learn how to effectively work with people, which is a critical skill in any business. Many of the techniques will likely surprise you.

5. *How To Write A Good Advertisement* – Victor Schwab

In business, you are going to have to learn effective ways of not just talking with people, but also writing emails, writing web content, making flyers, etc. This book will show you how.

www.ingramcontent.com/pod-product-compliance
Lightning Source LLC
Chambersburg PA
CBHW072047190526
45165CB00019B/2070